WOMEN
IN
SERICULTURE

WOMEN
IN
SERICULTURE

By
Dr. G. Sandhya Rani
Ph.D.
Associate Professor
Department of Women's Studies
Sri Padmavathi Mahila Visva Vidyalayam
Tirupathi (A.P.)
India

DISCOVERY PUBLISHING HOUSE
NEW DELHI-110002

First Published – 2006

Reprinted – 2024

ISBN: 978-81-8356-098-6

Women in Sericulture

Published by:

DISCOVERY PUBLISHING HOUSE

4383/4B, Ansari Road, Darya Ganj
New Delhi-110 002 (India)
Phone: +91-11-23279245; 23253475; 43596065
Mobile: +91 9811179893 / +91 9871656464
E-mail: discoverybooksindia@gmail.com
orderdphbooks@gmail.com
namitwasan9@gmail.com
web: www.discoverypublishinggroup.com

Printed at:
Infinity Imaging Systems
Delhi

Preface

Silk is the queen of textiles and occupies a prestigious place among all fibres. Sericulture has got great importance in our country since silk is very much imbibed into our traditions and culture.

The Indian sericulture Industry has taken giant strides during the last two decades. It has a very long history interwoven with Indian culture and civilization. India the biggest rawsilk consumer and the second largest producer of the world has unique distinction of being the only country producing all the four types of silk—Mulberry, Tasar, Eri and Muga.

The agro-climatic conditions are highly suitable to sericulture in India, besides, sericulture has been playing a very vital role in providing the much wanted rural employment. More than six million people are engaged in this industry of which 90 per cent are from the disadvantageous sector of the rural mass.

A few years ago sericulture has been considered a subsidiary occupation of poor farmers. But now with the continuous support of the Government of India has achieved the position of a main occupation in certain parts of the country.

In India, production of mulberry raw silk is mainly confined to the states of Karnataka, Andhra Pradesh, West Bengal, Tamil Nadu and Jammu and Kashmir which together account for 90 per cent of the country's total mulberry raw silk production. Next to Karnataka state, Andhra Pradesh is the leading silk producing state in India.

Andhra Pradesh though popularly known as 'River State' and 'Rice Bowl' of South India paradoxically, possesses widespread drought prone areas in Rayalaseema and Telangana regions due to scanty rainfall and its erratic distribution.

Rayalaseema Region in Andhra Pradesh state consists of four districts namely— Anantapur, Chittoor, Kurnool and Cuddapah. Though this region is known for frequent droughts and famines, it is rich in terms of the development of sericulture. As mulberry is drought resistant, sericulture has become the most promising activity to the formers in these four districts of Rayalaseema.

This region is showing enormous growth potential in sericulture, which in turn, improved the economic standards of the rural population. This has proved as the most suitable activity in providing gainful employment opportunities to both males and females. Women can themselves engage profitably in sericulture activities without going to farm.

Sericulture, being a family oriented occupation, women play a major role in various activities of the Industry. Nearly 60 per cent of the labour requirement is met by the women in general in almost all the traditional sericulture agencies.

Employment opportunities for women are also high in sericulture Industry. Various operations in the production of silk beneficially engage women in sericulture, because of its unique nature of work, proves to be an ideal activity for women who can work in addition to their regular tasks of taking care of the family. Its operation do not require hard labour. Almost all the sericulture activities, except such tasks digging, ploughing and carrying heavy loads, which are strenuous can be carried out by women independently. Silk-worms being delicate have to be handled with proper care. Thus the entire process of rearing needs expertise, high skill and patience. Women possess these qualities to an eminent degree and therefore and more suitable than men. It is worked out that about 2,575 women workdays comprising about 60 per cent are generated per annum out of a total of about 4,225 workdays in all the activities in sericulture per hectare of irrigated mulberry. Thus sericulture provides scope for the direct involvement of women in the process of production and decision making for improving their economic conditions and for giving them greater recognition and status in the family and society. Under the National Sericulture Project, the action plan on women envisages group-formation, special training programmes for women, allotment of land in the names of the women, special credit schemes for women etc. All these programmes are under implementation for raising the active participation of women in sericulture.

Sericulture has gained momentum during the last two decades and made remarkable progress. The Government of Andhra Pradesh through the implementation of a variety of programmes encouraging farmers to take up this occupation. Especially women are given special training, assistance, and encouragement in this activity. Women Development programmes include:

1. Formation of women groups to provide financial assistance for ensuring mutual support and to enhance their status in the household, community in terms of decision making and control over resources and benefit derived from such sources.

2. Training to women in new technologies to improve their technical knowledge and to improve the productivity.

Women's position and patience make silk worm handling easier—Moreover the aim of our planners and policy makers to provide gainful employment opportunities to women is fulfilled with the enormous expansion of sericulture and silk industry in this region.

Like nurturing family, their involvement in sericulture is also highly significant and needs a special mention. National Sericulture Project recognised their achievements and the year 1994 was declared as 'Year of Women in Sericulture'.

The main objective of this present study is to examine the growth of sericulture in Rayalaseema Region and its role in generation of employment opportunities for rural women in this region. The study is confined to four Rayalaseema districts (Anantapur, Chittoor, Kurnool and Cuddapah). To keep the study within the manageable limits without affecting adversely the investigation, the study was carried out in two mandals from each district, i.e. Anantapur and Hindupur and Anantapur district, Chandragiri and Palamaneru from Chittoor district, Atmakur and Emmiganur from Kurnool district and Rayachoti and Lakkireddy Palli from Cuddapah district.

Women occupy 50 per cent of the total population in these districts. Nearly 70 per cent of women depend on agriculture as agricultural labourers for their livelihood. The literacy rate among women was very low.

The study is based on both primary and secondary data. The study has highlighted the role of women in a variety of sericulture activities and also brought to light the inadequacies in production and marketing of the produce of Sericulturists.

The analytical and empirical investigations carried out in the four Rayalaseema districts reveal several interesting factors. This study has provided basis for offering specific suggestions for the development of sericulture in general and for increasing the participation of women in particular.

The working days generated in an acre of mulberry garden both for males and females was studied. In one acre of mulberry garden and for rearing 200-250 dfls on an average 338 man-days were generated, out of which 205 (61.5%) are female working days. The study reveals that 3113 to 4725 working days have been generated in Anantapur, Chittoor, Kurnool and Cuddapah districts on an average per hectare out of which female labour involvement was from 1,900 to 2,562 working days in study area.

The generation of employment opportunities for women are more in the study area when compared to men and ranged between 45 to 61 per cent in both mulberry cultivation and silk worm rearing.

As a growing enterprise sericulture is not free from problems. Therefore, stability is the immediate need of this industry. Price stability and timely availability of market information increases the involvement of women in more numbers.

This study is a clear distribution to understand the importance of sericulture in our rural economy. This also offers a new vision and various dimensions in rural development and women's role and their contributions to our economic development.

This book is divided into seven chapters. In the first chapter the importance of sericulture in Indian Economy and its suitability has been highlighted. The second chapter deals with the basic literature and the status of sericulture in Andhra Pradesh.

The third chapter is concerned with the development of sericulture in Rayalaseema and an empirical account of the socio-economic conditions of sample farmers. The fourth chapter analyses the economic structure of different activities of sericulture. The fifth chapter presents a clear picture of employment generation for rural women through sericulture.

The sixth chapter explains the problems of sericulturists with special reference to output, employment, marketing and extension. The last chapter brings out the summary and broad conclusions of the study.

This study is a clear contribution to understand the importance of sericulture in our rural economy. This also offers a new vision and various dimensions in rural development and women's role and their contributions to our economic development.

B. Venkateswarlu

Acknowledgements

In carrying out the present project work and bringing out to a successful completion, I have received generous help from a number of people. I place on record here my indebtedness to all of them.

I express my sincere thanks to the University Grants Commission, New Delhi for giving me this opportunity by providing financial assistance in carrying out this project work.

I deem it my duty as well as pleasure to express my sincere thanks to the authorities of Sri Padmavathi Mahila Visvavidyalayam, Tirupati for permitting me to conduct this study providing me with all the required facilities throughout the project work.

My sincere thanks are due to Prof. K.A. Parvathy, Head, Department of Women's Studies for her valuable suggestions in carrying out this work. I also express my deep sense of thanks to all my colleagues in the Department of Women's Studies for their encouragement and co-operation in this endeavour.

My special thanks are due to the Commissioner of Sericulture, Government of Andhra Pradesh, Hyderabad and also the Deputy Director of Sericulture in Anantapur, Kurnool, Cuddapah and Chittoor providing the necessary and valuable information.

I am grateful to the Library Staff of Sri Padmavathi Mahila Visvavidyalayam for having helped me by providing necessary material in execution of the project work.

I express my sincere thanks to all the sample farmers, without whose valuable co-operation, this endeavour could not have been completed.

My thanks are due to Ms. Jayalakshmi, Project Fellow, for her co-operation and assistance in collection of necessary information.

I am thankful to Dr. K.V.S. Sharma, Professor of Statistics, S.V. University, Tirupati for his valuable help in the interpretation of data formulation and adoption of the relevant statistical methods.

Last but not least I express my sincere thanks to Sri P. Karthik, Nithin Karthik Xerox, Tirupati for typing out the whole project report meticulously.

G. Sandhya Rani

Contents

1

Introduction

Women in India have been generally considered as "Home Makers" but not as those who also work for livelihood to support their families. They also form more than half of the agricultural labourers in India. Although, most Indian rural women spend 16 to 18 hours a day working at home and outside, their importance in the development of the family has not been fully recognised and appreciated. The basic fact is that the income generated by the rural women in the family is generally utilised more profitably for the socio-economic development of the family.

It is often seen that men migrate to the nearby urban areas in search of employment, leaving the entire burden of maintaining the household on women. If the rural households are to be made economically viable and self-sustaining units, the employment and income generation for rural women need to be given utmost priority. This can improve the socio-economic development of rural areas in a balanced manner. Infact, in developing countries like India, the economic status of rural women may be accepted as an index of the social development and the progress of the country.

Rural women have to be made economically self-dependent through the application of Science and Technology appropriate to the socio-economic conditions of the rural areas. While selecting programmes and technologies, all care be taken to ensure that these programmes enable the women to do productive work along with their family responsibilities. It is in this context that Sericulture has proved to be an excellent vocation for the development of the rural areas in India. Out of the total number of 5,75,700 villages in India, sericulture is being practised in about 45,000 villages, providing employment to about 5.15 million people.

Sericulture being an agro-based rural industry is highly suitable to the countries having an agricultural base and problems of providing employment to the rural landless labourers especially women. In fact, the silk production has brought advantages to small and marginal farmers in developing countries. It is mainly rural and labour intensive industry requiring relatively low investment and offering high profit potential and foreign exchange earnings. Mulberry leaf which is a feed to silkworms could be raised using the land unsuitable for other corps while waste by-products from sericulture can be of good value.

Sericulture being a family oriented occupation, women play a major role in various activities of the industry. Nearly 60 per cent of the labour requirement is met by the women in general in almost all the traditional sericulture agencies of the world. Women's precision and patience make silkworm handling easier. Traditions and customs of the society in Indian rural context do not encourage the majority of the rural women to work outdoors. Here sericulture proves to be a boon wherein women can carry all the work within the housing after attending to their own regular household chores. Thus sericulture is ideally suited for family women in the rural areas.

Sericulture, however, has emerged as the most appropriate labour intensive rural and semi-urban activity. This activity combines both agriculture and industry. Mulberry cultivation, silkworm rearing and cocoon production are agricultural activities whereas reeling, twisting, weaving and marketing are industrial activities. This enterprise starts in agriculture sector and ends in industrial sector. Sericulture, for example, played a very important role in transforming the traditional bound Japanese agriculture into a modernised agriculture by intensive use of land, labour and capital.

The importance of sericulture as an input for rural development has been recognised by the planners and it has been given due importance in sixth, seventh, eighth and ninth Five Year Plans of the country. Planners have come to the conclusion that there is a remote change of diverting rural population to urban areas for employment. At the same time land also cannot provide livelihood to the increasing population. Therefore, there are only the village industries which can contribute to employment. Handloom weaving is one of the them which has been recognised as an important traditional industry in India. Silk weaving in our country is mainly undertaken on handlooms.

India enjoys unique distinction in the field of sericulture as it is the only country producing all the four varieties (Mulberry, Tasar, Eri and Muga) of silk. Silks are differentiated into these four kinds depending upon the race, species of the worm and the food plants upon which they feed. What is commonly called as silk is 'mulberry silk'. The other three kinds if skills are called 'non-mulberry' silks or 'wild silks' as mulberry is not the food plant here.

Production of mulberry raw silk is mainly confined to the states of Karnataka, Andhra Pradesh, West Bengal, Tamil Nadu and Jammu and Kashmir which together account for 99 per cent of the country's total mulberry raw silk production. India is maintaining a steady upward trend in the output of natural raw silk and also in earning foreign exchange by exports of silk goods. During the year 1990-91, India earned Rs. 435.94 crores foreign exchange by exporting silk fabrics. India ranks second among the silk producing countries in the world next to China. Karnataka is the premier silk producing state of India. Next to Karnataka, Andhra Pradesh is the leading silk producing state in India. Although it is known as 'River State' and 'Rice Bowl' of South India with abundant water resources, paradoxically, it possess widespread drought prone areas in Rayalaseema and Telengana regions due to scanty rainfall and its erratic distribution.

After the constitution of a separate Department of Sericulture in 1980-81 and with the effective implementation of Drought Prone Areas Programme, mulberry sericulture and silk industries are showing enormous expansion in Rayalaseema Region of Andhra Pradesh. Silk industry has proved to be a money spinner for many middle class families in this region. With the evolving of silkworm races suitable for the tropical climatic conditions, the productivity of silk has increased and made this industry highly remunerative.

The aim of planners and policy makers to provide gainful employment opportunities to women is fulfilled with enormous expansion of sericulture and silk industry. In backward regions like Rayalaseema in Andhra Pradesh state where there are no alternative opportunities to undertake, women are actively employed in silk industry so as to raise their incomes and also health status of their families. Reeling, twisting and weaving are the activities in which women participation is high as they constitute two-thirds of the total persons engaged in various activities of silk industry right from mulberry cultivation down to weaving of silk fabrics.

Review of Literature

To discuss the relevance of the study, a brief review of literature is presented.

D.L. Narayana in his 'Economics of Sericulture in Rayalaseema (1979) presented an elaborate study on sericulture in the four Rayalaseema districts of A.P. According to his study sericulture is mainly concentrated in Chittoor and Anantapur districts. The book gives a detailed account of the economics of sericulture, the problems and also the scope for its development.

D.V. Ramana in his book, 'Economics of Sericulture and Silk Industry', (1980) gave a picture of sericulture covering both on-farm and off-farm activities. The analysis of the benefits of sericulture bringing out its importance in terms of income and employment generation is also presented.

S.B. Shantharaj Kumar in his book, 'Silk Handloom Industry in Andhra Pradesh', (1986) covered the pattern of work conditions of weavers, the process of manufacturing warp and weft.

In the book, 'Silk Industry, Problems and Prospects', Abdul Aziz and H.G. Hanumappa presented an overall picture of the prospects of silk industry and its problems.

Sanjay Sinha's book the 'Development of Indian Silk' gives a clear picture of sericulture in Indian economy. The products and production systems, the policy and micro economic issues in silk production are discussed in detail.

A.P. Raj Purohit and K.V. Govind Raju in their book titled, 'Employment and Income in Sericulture' presented sericulture as a tool which helps to increase employment opportunities in the economy. The creation of employment and income in silk reeling units is also dealt with.

T.D. Koshy, in his book, 'Silk Exports and development (1993), has tried to educate the silk exporter about the products they deal with Part-I of this book deals with various aspects of sericulture like silk production, processing and procurement and part-II is about silk trade and export procedures.

Sericulture for Rural Development (1986) edited by Hanumappa comprise eleven papers presented by eminent Professors and Scholars, which highlight sericulture in Karnataka right from mulberry cultivation down to research development and training activities. The book as a whole gives a clear picture of the role of sericulture in rural development.

P. Venkata Narasaiah in his book 'Sericulture in India' (1992) examines in detail the growth of sericulture in India. He points out that sericulture which is an agro-based cottage industry, fits very well in India's rural structure, where agriculture continues to be the main industry. This book contributes significantly to a better understanding of the strength and weaknesses of sericulture operations. It also offers some useful practical suggestions to overcome the various current problems and hindrances faced by the industry, and to ensure overall development.

The book 'Sericulture Society and Economy' (1993), edited by H.G. Hanumappa, is a volume of ten research papers by scholars engaged in studying the importance of sericulture to our economy and society. H.G. Hanumappa, who is principal contributor to the volume, presents sericulture as an economically rewarding enterprise. He says that sericulture, consisting of several sets of activities offers immense scope for social scientists to explore the interface that sericulture has with economics and society. These essays offer an insight into the processes by which rural development is taking place. The book is divided into two sections. The first section deals with the impact of sericulture on output, income, energy and rural institutions the second section consists of papers examining the socio-economic issues of the silk-reeling aspect of sericulture.

Dr. (Mrs) G. Ganga and Dr. (Mrs) J. Sulochana Chetty's book 'An Introduction to Sericulture' (1991), gives an overall idea of sericulture. In this book the authors discuss in detail the history of sericulture, the importance of sericulture and present a package of practices for mulberry cultivation. They also give an account of the diseases and pests generally to which silk worm are prone. The physiological aspects of silkworm were also given in detail.

The book 'Sericulture and Development' (1993), edited by J. Acharya gives a succinct report of his field studies in sericulture in the southern states of Karnataka, Andhra Pradesh and Tamil Nadu. The essays cover the whole gamut of issues concerning sericulture and development, women and children, technology and extension pattern of sericulture in different agro-climatic zones, problem of sericulture under water scarcity etc.

S.R. Charsley in his book, 'Culture and Sericulture', focused on livestock industry and sericulture based on agriculture, which in India have been subject to schemes of development intensively since early in this century.

L. Devasurappa in his paper, 'Silk Industry' gave an overall idea on the performance of silk industry in the Karnataka state. The various activities involved in sericulture commencing from mulberry cultivation to silk weaving are discussed in detail.

M. Prabha Sekhar and C. Ravi Kumar in their paper, 'Role of Women in Indian Sericulture' explained how rural women have to be made economically self-dependent through sericulture.

R.K. Datta and C. Ravi Kumar have analysed the role of sericulture in rural development in their paper, 'Sericulture and Rural Development'.

'Mulberry cultivation' by Boraiah covers not only mulberry silk but also eri, tasar, and muga silks. The author, however, gives top priority to mulberry cultivation and considers some ways of successful cultivation of mulberry gardens to obtain high productivity.

In the paper entitled 'Problems and Prospects of Sericulture' K.Periswamy discusses many problems of sericulture, commencing from mulberry cultivation to cocoon production. He suggests some techniques and measures to overcome these problems. He also gives an account of the status of sericulture in China, the leading country in mulberry production.

Apart from these, 'The Central Silk Board', Bangalore. The Central Sericultural Research and Training Institute, Mysore and 'National Institute of Rural Development, Hyderabad have conducted many workshops, seminars and surveys on sericulture development and published their reports. These reports are highly useful to formulate an idea of the growth potential of sericulture in Andhra Pradesh and India.

Importance and Scope of the Study

As sericulture industry can be broadly classified into mulberry cultivation, silkworm rearing, post-cocoon process and manufacturing of rearing appliances, almost all activities in sericulture are carried out by women except some which are shared along with men. However, there are certain jobs like weeding, leaf harvest, silk reeling which are exclusive monopoly of women. Thus about 2562 women work days comprising about 61 per cent are generated in all the activities in sericulture per hectare of irrigated mulberry per annum out of a total of about 4225 work days. Thus during the first year of establishment, it generates about 5.8 work years for women, out of a total of 9.5 work years per hectare under irrigated conditions. On the other hand, after the establishment (third year onwards), 7.0 work years are generated for women, out of a total of 11.5 work years under irrigated mulberry.

Apart from the above activities, the women are also employed in various activities of silkworms, egg production and also in moth examination for detection of diseases. Besides, indirect employment is also generated on many other activities of the silk industry.

As most of the studies conducted so far have emphasised the economies of sericulture and silk industry and their prospects and problems, specific aspects of employment generation for women have not studied so far although general picture is brought out in some studies.

The present study focuses its attention on identifying the crucial aspects of employment generation for rural women in sericulture in drought prone areas with special reference to Rayalaseema region of Andhra Pradesh. The socio-economic issues such as lack of regular employment opportunities to the landless women; non-participation of women in marketing though women are constantly involved in almost all activities upto the production of cocoons; general issues like inequality between men and women labour as there is no equality between men and women with respect to job opportunity, rights and wages since female workers always get less wages than a male would get for the same work; and lack of training programmes, exposure to improved technology, extension services to the women on par with men though there is fullest involvement of women in most of the sericulture activities.

The study is conducted in a micro-framework. As it is an empirical study, the quantitative and qualitative aspects of women employment and shifts in the occupational structure are analysed. The four districts of Rayalaseema namely Anantapur, Chittoor, Kurnool and Cuddapah are covered to bringout the analysis on the economics of sericulture, income and employment generation, marketing etc., and problems of sericulture in the selected areas.

Objectives of the Study

The study covers the following specific objectives to understand and analyse the growth of sericulture and its role in the generation of employment for rural women in Rayalaseema region:

1. To examine the economics of sericulture in general in A.P. and Rayalaseema region in particular;
2. To study the economic structure of the different activities of sericulture and their prospects;
3. To analyse the level of employment generation for women in rural areas in sericulture and its impact on rural development; and
4. To examine the specific problems of sericulture with reference to rearing of cocoons, marketing, financial assistance etc.

Hypotheses

The following specific hypotheses are formulated to meet the above objectives of the study:

1. Sericulture is providing stable income and employment to many rural agricultural families and a livelihood to scores of landless farm and non-farm women labourers giving much economic strength;
2. The role of women in the process of sericulture development has increased as employment generation for women is more than men in mulberry cultivation and silkworm rearing;
3. The benefits of sericulture are not fully reaching the family for the socio-economic upliftment as the women are not involved in marketing and financial transactions.

Methodology

Keeping in view the specific set of objectives as listed, an indepth study of sericulture development in Rayalaseema region has been attempted. Here methodology needs special mention. The study is based on collection of data from both secondary and primary sources in the four districts of the region.

(a) Sampling Design

The sampling design is formulated for the purpose of the collection of primary data. Stratified random sampling method is adapted for collecting primary data by designing the sample from the population. Sericulture is now practised in almost all the mandals of Rayalaseema region. Since it is not possible to cover all the mandals in this inquiry and to keep the study within manageable limits without in anyway minimizing its significance eight mandals (at the rate of two mandals from each district) have been selected as the study area. They are Anantapur and Hindupur mandals from Anantapur district, Emmiganur and Atmakur mandals from Kurnool district, Rayachoti and Lakki Reddy Palli from Cuddapah district and Chandragiri and Palamaneru from Chittoor district. Within the study area again eight villages at the rate of one village from each mandal have been selected;

Rachanapalli and Kotnur from Anantapur and Hindupur mandals, Karivena and Jalimanchi from Atmakur and Emmiganur mandals. Kuruvapalli and Ganganapalli from Rayachoti and Lakki Reddi Palli mandals and Gangundra palli and Baripalli from Chandragiri and Palamaneru mandals respectively.

(b) Collection of Data

Secondary data relating to the different aspects of sericulture are collected from the Chief Planning Officer, Dept. of Statistics, and Dept. of Sericulture etc. The information regarding various allied activities of sericulture are collected from the offices of DRDA, Handlooms and Textile Board and Khadi and Village Industries Board, DIC etc. The studies and reports brought out by the Ministry of Textiles, ISEC and Central Silk Board, Bangalore and its constituents and other published reports, books, articles in journals and district Gazetteers are also referred to draw secondary data.

Primary data was collected from the sample households by adopting the method of Direct Personal Interviews with the head of the family. To elicit the required information, a well structured questionnaire was designed with probing questions. The questionnaire is divided into broad sections viz., (i) Identification, (ii) Socio-economic data, (iii) Structure of income and employment for women in particular, (iv) economic structure of enterprise (v) financial sources and marketing of output and(vi) problems of sericulture.

(c) Analysis of Data

The collected data is analysed and tabulated. A cross-sectional analysis among the various allied activities of silk industry is studied and the size, quantum of employment and output data is subjected to statistical analysis. The relationship among these variables is studied using appropriate statistical techniques. Apart from tabulation and analysis, necessary graphs are incorporated in the study.

(d) Statistical Tools Used

The data collected has been analysed using SPSS10.0. The specific tools used are cross tabulations, percentages, averages, growth analysis (linear and compound growthrates) fitting of trend lines etc., The facilities available in MS Excel have also been utilised for statistical analysis. Excel graphs have been used to demonstrate the trends whereever applicable.

Chapter Scheme

The entire study is divided into seven chapters and a brief description of each chapter is presented here.

In the first chapter which is introductory the importance of sericulture in Indian Economy and its suitability has been highlighted. The review of relevant literature, the methodology adopted and hypotheses formulated have been pointed out.

The second chapter is concerned with the basic literature and the status of sericulture in Andhra Pradesh.

The third chapter deals with the development of sericulture in Rayalaseema and an empirical account of the socio-economic conditions of farmers engaged in sericulture in the selected villages of the region.

The fourth chapter analyses the economic structure of different activities of sericulture.

The fifth chapter presents a clear picture of employment generation for rural women through various activities of sericulture.

The sixth chapter explains the problems of sericulturists with special reference to output employment, marketing and extension.

The last chapter brings out the summary and broad conclusions of the study.

2

Progress of Sericulture in Andhra Pradesh

Today sericulture shows a picture of well knit agro-based, labour intensive cottage industry in the world. The final product of sericulture i.e., silk can be produced and marketed where climatic conditions are favourable and labour is cheap and abundant. In that way sericulture is one of the most labour intensive activities combining both agriculture and industry. This chapter is divided into three sections for presenting the data in a detailed form. A brief account of the history of sericulture is furnished in the Section one. In section two an attempt is made to present a detailed picture of the progress of sericulture in Andhra Pradesh. Section three deals with the involvement of women in sericulture.

'Silk' is the queen of textiles as it occupies a prestigious place among all fibres. It is famous for its lustrous look and soft feel. Moreover, it is one of the strongest fibre, two thirds as strong as a steel wire, but one of the delicate and lightest. The origin of the silk is so ancient and according to the records this silk industry undoubtedly originated in China and achieved improvement in the Chinese economy during the period of emperor "Haung Ti" (2640 BC). It is believed that "Si Ling Shi", wife of emperor "Haung Ti" made silk fashionable by showing her personal attention.[1] Silk was used as medium of exchange during that period.

In India sericulture is an ancient industry dating back to atleast second century B.C.[2] The ancient Indian Sanskrit literature like "Amarakosha" confirms that the origin of silk industry as China.

Silk was called "cheenaum-sokam' or "cloth-china" in some of the older Sanskrit works.[3] It is believed that the silkworm eggs and mulberry seeds were carried to India by a Chinese Princess from a province near Indian border.

In its long history, sericulture faced booms and busts during its travel towards prosperity. Efforts were made in the 18th, 19th and 20th centuries, during British rule to patronise silk mainly by the British traders. It actually flourished in the sates of the then Bengal, Mysore and Kashmir. Though sericulture suffered a series of setbacks briefly staged a come back during the second world war period. When the second world was ended in the mid 1940s silk industry slumped and silk consumption ceased abruptly.[4]

Thanks to the devotion of the Government of India and the measures it took to encourage sericulture in the country. After 1945 sericulture industry once again entered the period of prosperity. It has attained rapid progress especially during the last two decades and since then it has really come of age and is now poised for a great leap forward.

Advantages of Sericulture

A few years back sericulture was considered a subsidiary occupation of poor farmers, while the big landlords used to cultivate only food crops, fruits, orchards etc. Now sericulture is no longer a subsidiary occupation and more and more farmers including the big landlords are taking up. The various advantages of sericulture already identified are as follows:

1. Sericulture is a labour intensive rural industry creating employment to 12 to 15 persons per hectare of mulberry;
2. It requires low gestation period and mulberry plantation starts yielding just in five to six months after raising mulberry;
3. Sericulture requires low investment and once the plantation is established it will continue to yield for 12 to 15 years with little expenditure on maintenance and gives higher returns which is around Rs.40,000/- per hectare of irrigated mulberry per annum. Sericulture involves simple technologies, easy to understand and

adopt even by illiterate farmers and it gives returns in quick succession yielding income in every two to three months;

4. It does not involve hard labour and rearing of silkworm is generally attended to by women and old people;
5. It does not require sophisticated machinery and involves use of simple appliances;
6. Mulberry plants can be grown on any type of soil even in forest fringes, hill slopes and watershed areas;
7. Sericulture ideally suits even in rainfed conditions because of its low cost of production and higher returns than any other dry crop;
8. Mulberry plant withstands severe drought conditions and gives atleast some income for sustenance while other agricultural crops wither away.

Therefore, sericulture would be a more advantageous industry for improving the economy of retarded sections of the society like Scheduled Castes and Scheduled Tribes. Non-mulberry sericulture is largely practised by tribals. It ideally suits for small and marginal farmers owning less than one hectare of mulberry plantation. Its' by products like mulberry twigs, silkworm litter, pupa pierced and unreelable cocoons, reeling waste etc. are also useful in one form or other and gives income. Sericulture provides self-employment to the educated unemployed youth in its different sectors. It also creates employment opportunities in the allied industries like manufacture of appliances, machineries etc. Raw silk products have very good demand both in domestic and International markets. Thus it is a good source of earnings of foreign exchange.[5]

Basics of Sericulture

Sericulture means raising of mulberry, the food plant and rearing of silkworms for production of silk. Silks are differentiated into four kinds depending upon the race, species of the worm and the food plant upon which they feed. They are (a) Tasar or Tussar, (b) Eri, (c) Muga and (d) Mulberry. The first three kinds of silks are called 'non-mulberry' silks as mulberry is not the food plant for the worms. These are also called 'wild silks' since the worms are not fully domesticated unlike mulberry worms and are practised in forests and hilly areas.

(a) Tasar Silk

'Tasar silk' or 'Tassar silk' is produced by a species called "Antheeraca Mylitta". This exists in the form of nearly 19 ecotypes thriving between 450-750 metres above Mean Sea Level (MSL). It is a wild species found in Uni, bi and trivoltines. It is polyphagous in nature. The main food plants are Asan, Arjun and Sal. Tasar is copperish coloured silk and does not possess the lusture of mulberry silk. A new strain of Tasar worm has been developed from "Antherea royelie' and "Antherea pernyi" which feed on Oak trees abounding at 600-1800mm above MSL. Oak, Tasar silk is yellow to white in colour, the finest in non-mulberry silks. Tasar culture is found in Bihar, Orissa, Madhya Pradesh, Karnataka and Andhra Pradesh.

(b) Eri Silk

Eri silk is also known as 'Endi' and ranks next to 'Tasar' in commercial importance. The genus "philosamia' comprises 17 species distributed mainly in 'Indo-Australian region'. The silk worm(phelosamia Rivoini) thrives in India and is multivoltine, yielding four to six crops a year. The food of eri silk worm is castor leaves, papaya and payam. Eri cocoons are white and brick red in colour. The eri culture is found in Orissa, Bihar, West Bengal, Madhya Pradesh, Karnataka and Andhra Pradesh.

(c) Muga Silk

Muga is obtained from worms 'Antherea Asamensis"which are polyphagous primarily feeding on som and soalu. The silk is golden yellow to creamy white in colour with lustrous look. Muga silk is the monopoly of Assam in the world. It is also found in Meghalaya.

(d) Mulberry Silk

What is commonly called as silk is mulberry silk. "Bombyx mori" a native of northern China or Bengal is the silk worm which produces mulberry silk. It is found in all voltines. Mulberry sericulture is also known as Mori culture. It dominates the other silks in various aspects of production and popularity. Mulberry sericulture is being practised in various states of India. It consists of four operations. (a) Mulberry cultivation (b) Silkworm rearing, (c) Mounting or Cocoon production, (d) Silkworm egg production.

Mulberry Cultivation

Mulberry cultivation is an agricultural operation. Mulberry plant is hard and can survive in severe drought conditions also. It responds well to the quality and efficiency of operations and leaf yield is also very high. It can also be grown as bush, high bush, medium bush or tree. In Andhra Pradesh mulberry is grown in bush form upto 1.50 to 2.10m. and exists for 15 years. Mulberry plant yields leaf within four to five months after plantation under irrigated conditions. Bush mulberry can be grown from cuttings, seeds, seedlings and root-stock. As it is a perennial crop, it needs manual attention throughout the year. The leaf yield of mulberry plantation varies enormously basing on the inputs. It ranges from 3,000 to 10,000 kg under rainfed conditions and from 10,000 to 40,000 kg under irrigated conditions per hectare.[6]

Silkworm Rearing

Silkworm rearing is a cottage activity. The sericulturist rears silkworms either in his own house or in a separate shed built for this purpose. This activity needs much manual attention and skill. There are four silkworm races viz., univoltine, bivoltine, trivoltine and multi-voltine. In univoltine the silk worm passes through only one cycle in a year and remains dormant in the egg stage or in the pupa stage in the cocoon for a long time, that is having only one breed or generation within a year. The multivoltine has cycles after cycles, where a cycle just takes only six weeks. The univoltines are very sensitive to high temperature and reared in cooler regions. The cocoons are bigger in size and possess more silk. The multivoltines are suitable to warm regions and many rearings can be had in a year. But the size and the quality of the cocoon is low. Bivoltine and trivoltine fall in between these two.

The silkworm undergoes four distinct stages—egg, larva, pupa and moth-during its life cycle. The mothlays eggs. From the eggs tiny ant like worms hatch out and feed on mulberry leaves. This is the second stage called larva or caterpillar. The larva when fully grows spins silk into a cocoon around itself. Inside the cocoon the worm transforms into pupa develops into a moth which is the final stage. This moth comes out of the cocoon. After copulation the female moth lays eggs. The life cycle is thus repeated. The length of the cycle differs from region to region and from one species to another depending on factors like climate, vegetation and temperature.

The sericulturist purchases eggs or disease tree layings (dfls) or industrial seeds generally from government grainages or licensed seed products. Per each laying there should be 350-400 eggs. The eggs are white or whitish yellow in colour. These eggs hatch within nine or ten days after their laying. Tiny ant like worms come out of shells. Each larva is few milli meters long and weighs about 0.5 mg. The mulberry leaves are cut into finest pieces and sprinkled over the larvae. The larvae are fed for about 24-25 days. As the worms grow, they are fed with bigger and bigger leaf bits. Four to eight feeds are given in a day.

During the larva stage the silkworm moults four times. Moutling is a process where the silkworm casts of its existing skin in place of new one. The period before or after moulting is called 'instar'. There are five instars in a silkworms life. During IV and V instars 90-95 per cent of the mulberry will be given as food. By the end of V instar, the caterpillar increases its weight 10,000 times showing a weight of four to five grams. Proper care should be taken during IV moult. The IV moulting duration compared to the first three is slightly prolonged and takes nearly 30 hours under optimum conditions of temperature (24°C) and humidity (60-70 R.H).

The larvae are fed both by leaf and shoot harvest. During early stages, the larvae are fed only with leaf and by both leaf and shoot during the IV and V stages. The rearing bed spacing of 0.06 sq.m. is recommended for 100dfts, in the beginning. During IV and V instars bed area should be increased in proportion to the growth of silkworm larvae. Bed cleaning should be done every day. This should be done with nylon or cotton nets of appropriate mesh size. Heavy crop losses are recorded due to infections, flacherie, bacterial flacherie, nuclear pllyhedros's etc. Pebrine and Muscardine also occur occasionally. Crops are also damaged due to uzy fly. It is a problem which causes major crop loss. So silkworm rearing under nylon nets has become compulsory.

Mounting (Cocoon Production)

In this process matured silkworms are kept in a proper frame to facilitate spinning of cocoons. Such frames are called 'mountages'. The V instar larvae, after completion of 5th-7th day depending upon the variety of silkworm become ripe for spinning. They should be picked up and placed on the mountages in right time to avoid silk wastage. Worms pre-matured or too late after riping can give poor quality of cocoons. Moreover humidity, ventilation and temperature also influence cocoon quality. Temperature should be around 23°C with 60-70 per cent R.H., and continuous air current during cocooning are found optimum.

Mountages used in India ranges from simple dried grass and twigs in Assam, dried mulberry twigs in Jammu and Kashmir to bamboo spirals popularly called 'Chandrikas' in all southern states and West Bengal. Mounting and harvesting is difficult in the first two types requiring much labour and also results in more double and deformed cocoons. Bamboo mountage with one fourth square inch holes in the back side mat was found the best with least double and urinated cocoons, higher reliability and better raw silk recovery. "Plastic collapsible" mountage for its convenience of handling and storage and "Bottle brush" mountage for its low cost are also popular.

The ripe worms must be mounted at the rate of 440 to 660 worms per square metre depending upon silk worm variety. This helps to obtain good cocoon build, lesser double cocoon and lesser urinated cocoons. Thus in 2.4x1.6m Chandrikas about 1,000 worms of bivoltine 1,200 worms of multi x bi-voltine and 1,400 worms of PmXC niche cross can be mounted.

Spinning of cocoons will be completed in two to three days. The worm inside the cocoon turns into pupa on the fourth or fifth day depending upon the silkworm variety. So cocoons should be harvested for marketing only on the fifth day for multinbivoltine or sixth day for bivoltine from the day of spinning. On this day, pupa is hard and cocoon shell is dry and suitable for long distance transportation for marketing.

Cocoon yield will be 40 to 45 kg in multi x biovoltine and 50 kg in bivolting hybrid for 100 layings. Generally 20 kg of leaf should result in 1 kg of cocoon. If all the rearing conditions are good, more efficient ratio in the range of 16 to 18 should be possible.[7] It is said that a silkworm can yield 800m. length yarn during its life time.

Cocoon yield depends on the production of silkworm eggs. The seed organisation plays a vital role on which the success of industry depends. The layings are called disease free layings (dfls) since care has to be taken that the layings are healthy and free from any disease or infection after microscope tests. The establishment where the layings are produced is called a grainage. Generally rearers use cross breed layings produced from the multivoltine local race (LR) and female foreign race (FR). The FR and LR dfls are also called basic seed and are produced by Government in their respective grainages. These dfls are supplied to notified reares for further multiplication. These rearers breed the dfls and sell the resultant seed cocoons to the government grainages. In the cross breed grainages the commercial seed is produced by cross breeding.

Employment Generation

At present, sericulture provides employment to around six million persons in India and most of them belong to the weaker sections of society. It can be said that no other single activity, whether agricultural or industrial, can bring such fortune to the most needy.

A farm labourer is able to find employment all the year round by combining mulberry cultivation with silkworm rearing. Since Indian agriculture is seasonal in character attention should be given to this aspect of employment in agriculture. In controlling unemployment and seasonal unemployment, sericulture can play an efficient and a relevant role.

The nature of employment in sericulture industry can be divided into two types: (1) Agricultural—includes mulberry cultivation, silkworm rearing, Cocoon production; and (2) Industrial—includes reeling of cocoons, twisting, warping, dyeing and weaving. The former activities are rural in nature and the latter are semi-urban and urban.

As a labour intensive export-oriented cottage industry sericulture can generate, high employment and income per unit area of land. One hectare of mulberry plantation under irrigation generates about 13 work years annually in mulberry cultivation, silkworm rearing, silk reeling, twisting and weavings.[8]

The labour requirements in sericulture is more than two and half times that of paddy and ten times that of groundnut. Thus the employment generation in sericulture is very high over that of the other crops, including paddy and groundnut which are taken as double crops in a year.

Involvement of Family Labour

The utilisation of family labour reduces the production cost considerably and increase the profit substantially. In the Rayalaseema Region of Andhra Pradesh the participation of family labour in mulberry cultivation and silkworm rearing is worked out to be around 68 per cent.[9] However, the Central Sericultural Research and Training Institute, Mysore, in its study of "social and economic changes among sericulturists in 1983-84" found that the share of family labour in the production of mulberry and cocoon is gradually decreasing.[10]

Indirect Employment Effects

The whole area of raw silk industry in the broadest sense will also provide new employment. In silk reeling activity there is a considerable scope for generation of employment opportunities to the artisans and unskilled workers of rural areas.[11] A reeler, with a unit of 10 basins, provides employment, to 21 persons including the reeler. The organisation of reeling and silk weaving can also help some of the markets and most vulnerable sections of society in rural areas. Silk waste and pupae, the byproducts of silk industry, open yet another sector of economic activities keeping people busy in processing and spinning of silk waste, producing pupae oil and pupae meal.

The mulberry cultivation, which requires more and better silkworm races as well as increased production of mulberry seed, should be a source of considerable indirect stimulus to employment. If the job opportunities created in the construction of irrigation wells, rearing houses, repair and replacement of rearing equipment, reeling, marketing, transport extension, research, etc., with all their forward and backward linkages are also considered, the employment potential of sericulture will be seen to be enormous.

High Income Generator

Sericulture is a highly remunerative cash crop with the rich dividends. It is the only cash crop which provides frequent and attractive returns in the tropical states of the country throughout the year. The average annual income per hectare would be around Rs. 40,000/- per hectare which is substantially high when compared to that of the other tropical crops. Sericulture industry is, therefore, well suited to the small and marginal farmers who are the below poverty line. Another plus point is that the plantation takes deep roots and survives in severe drought conditions. As a drought resistant plant, mulberry is highly preferred in drought affected areas.

The silk industry plays a vital role in transferring wealth from the richer sections of society to the poorer sections. Silk is consumed mostly by the affluent and the money spent by them on the purchase of silk is distributed among the sericulturists, reelers, twisters, weavers and traders. The details of the distribution of income from the sale of soft silk fabric among different sections of society are shown below in Table—2.1 and depicted in Graph—2.1. From the Table 2.1 it may be seen that the cocoon producer receives nearly 52 to 57 per cent of the money from the sale of silk fabric.

Table—2.1 Distribution of income from sale of soft silk fabric

Sl. No.	*Category of Persons*	*Soft Silk Fabric of*		
		40 gms/m.	*50 gms/m.*	*60 gms/m.*
1.	Cocoon Producer	51.5	54.6	56.8
2.	Reeler	6.2	6.6	6.8
3.	Twister	8.3	8.7	9.1
4.	Weaver	14.5	12.3	10.7
5.	Trader	19.5	17.8	16.6
	Total	**100.00**	**100.00**	**100.00**

Source: Silk in India-Statistical Biennial, Central Silk Board, Bangalore, 1988.

Graph—2.1

Distribution of income from sale of soft silk fabric (60 gms/m)

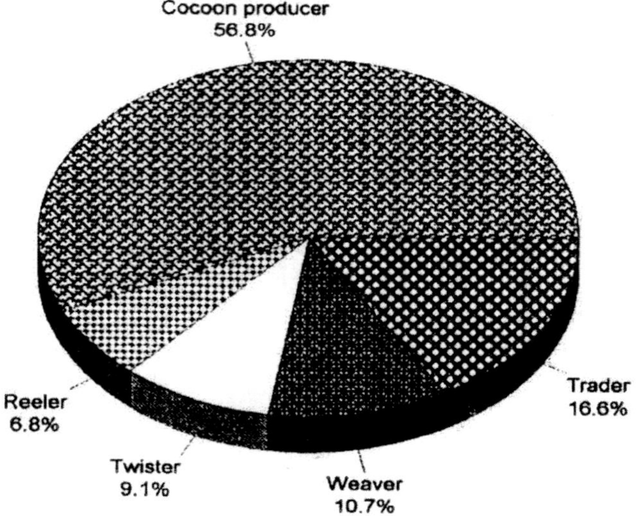

By Products of Sericulture

In sericulture nothing goes waste. Its by-products are useful in many ways. Mulberry leaves and shoots left by the silkworms form good fodder to the cattle and increases markedly their milk yield. The stifled and much maligned pupae are used in the preparation of dog biscuits, oil, etc. The oil and the protein powder extracted from the dead pupae can be utilized in manufacturing soaps and baking industries respectively. It forms a rich food in poultry, fishery and piggery. The silkworm's excreta can be used as manure. The rational utilisation and disposal of by-products helps the sericulturists to enhance their economic gains.

Considering the above advantages of sericulture it should be an effective tool for rural development. In view of its high employment potential and remunerative income generation, sericulture is regarded as one of the important means of alleviating rural poverty and ushering in rural prosperity, and therefore, receiving due attention in the rural development programmes at the State and Central levels.[12] The National Commission on

Agriculture has also rightly observed that large-scale expansion of this industry would substantially benefit the vast number of small and marginal farmers besides providing employment opportunities for millions in the rural sector.[13]

Role of Sericulture in the Development of Rural Sector

It is rightly said that sericulture is a boon to rural farmers. It plays an unique role in the development of rural economy. Its uniqueness lies in the fact that its activities not only engage the rural households in the cultivation of mulberry and silkworm rearing but also encompass in their fold a whole range of reelers and weavers.

A large section of farmers with uneconomical holdings and an enormous group of ruined artisans who constitute the bulk of the non-agricultural section of the rural population together tell the tragic tale of these sections of the rural population in the India.

During the last 30 years there has been a considerable growth of industries in India, but it has hardly improved the standard of life, more especially in the rural areas. The industrial growth has been slow and lopsided, and a few large scale industries are concentrated in the cities.

As India lives in her villages and agriculture is the backbone of her economic life, all efforts must devote to solve the rural economic problems. Agriculture in India is not a business proposition for our farmers but a way of life. But many economic forces such as the steady increase in population, decay of indigenous industries, lack of other avenues of employment and the rise in land values, have been responsible for this increasing pressure on land.

This increasing pressure of population on the soil and the growing indebtedness of the agricultural classes due to a combination of factors has led to the emergence of a class of landless labourers. These labourers may be classified into three groups: (1) field labourers—who comprise ploughman, reapers, sowers, weeders, etc; (2) ordinary labourers—who are engaged in such works as embankment, well digging and canal silt clearing, (3) skilled labourers such as carpenters, masons, blacksmiths and leather workers and such other artisans who, though not exclusively agricultural workers, are engaged for important purposes by the farmer, and the wages paid to them are governed by those paid to the agricultural labourers in the village. It is also to be noted that in rural areas the agricultural labourer is not only unemployed over a considerable part of the year but the wages paid to him even during the period of employment are very low. The labourer's earning power is very low and in some parts of India his extreme indebtedness has driven him to work as a bonded-labourer in the fields of his creditor.

India has been an agricultural country in the past and will continue to be so in the future, although its industrial development has been quite spectacular in recent years. According to the estimates by 2001 A.D, the population would reach 986 million. Then the pressure of population on land would increase enormously resulting in further lowering of standards in agricultural production. Excessive pressure on land leads to high rate of poverty, disguised unemployment, under-employment, etc.[14]

Role of Sericulture in Rural Development

As noted already sericulture has a great potential to alleviate rural poverty and unemployment. Mulberry, as a drought resistant plant, could be grown even in areas with low rainfall. It has wider scope for augmenting family income and employment opportunities for small and marginal farmers. It would create employment opportunities all through the year on farm and off-farm ranging from cultivation of mulberry and rearing of silkworms to allied activities.

Compared to other crops, the work participation rate is quite high in sericulture. It also absorbs many non-cultivators in the process of picking of leaves, rearing of silkworms and other allied activities. The migration of unskilled labour is a common feature in rural areas. But sericulture not only provides income for sericulturists but also retains people from mass migration to other places in search of employment.

Sericulture could be taken up in all kinds of regions. Appropriate technologies are now available for growing mulberry under all kinds of agro climatic conditions. In fact, in some of the traditional rainfed sericulture areas where even millets could grow only with difficulty, the rearing of local race silkworms with local variety of mulberry has provided a survival strategy for generations of small and marginal farmer households.

The highly intensive nature of sericulture makes it particularly suitable for the marginal and small economic groups to take it up on a sustainable basis. Rearing of silkworms is always more profitable with family labour than with hired labour. Wage workers prefer to work in silkworm rearing rather than in agricultural farm work. In reeling, the work-load is heavy and the wage rates are also higher than in any other farm work or other comparable industries. Thus sericulture provides an opportunity to the poorer sections of society to participate in the process of economic development.

Sericulture provides a means of regular and stable income with a high annual turnover of three to four crops in rainfed conditions and five to six crops under irrigated conditions. Division of the garden into plots with alternate harvest timings, could enable the sericulturists to carry on silkworm rearing throughout the year continuously. Thus a regular and steady income from sericulture helps the poor to improve their standard of living.

Growth of Sericulture in Andhra Pradesh

Sericulture has a long history in Karnataka State. Andhra Pradesh ranks next to Karnataka in mulberry raw silk production. A major portion of India's mulberry raw silk comes from these two states only. Thus sericulture has come to play a unique role in the rural economies of Andhra Pradesh especially in Rayalaseema region. In the following pages a brief account about the growth of sericulture in Andhra Pradesh in general and in Rayalaseema region in particular has been presented.

Progress of Sericulture in Andhra Pradesh

Andhra Pradesh is the fifth biggest state in India both in terms of area (2.74 ,400 km) and population.[15] It consists of 23 districts, four in Rayalaseema, ten in Telangana and nine in Coastal Andhra. Sericulture is ideally suited to a predominantly agricultural state like Andhra Pradesh. The main concentration has been in the Rayalaseema region of the state where climatic conditions are suitable for this activity. Andhra Pradesh produces both mulberry and tasar silk.

Andhra Pradesh has achieved the second place in the production of mulberry raw silk, although it had no place in the sericulture map of India when the state was formed in 1956. The hectarage under mulberry cultivation in 1953 was just two hectares which reached to 16 hectares by 1956.[16] Andhra Pradesh was not a traditional state of sericulture and was a new entrant into the sericulture enterprise. But within four decades due to enormous progress of sericulture in it, the state has achieved the distinction of second place in India's mulberry raw silk production and now it is being treated as one of the traditional states of sericulture in the country.

Palamaneru in the Chittoor district was the only sericulture farm formerly. Gradually owing to the efforts of Sri S.V. Ramamurthy, adviser to the Governor of the then Madras province, sericulture spread to Hindupur, Araku and other places. Sericulture came to be practised in a small way with the setting up of a few farms by the Government at Lepakshi. Bhadrachalam, Chintalapudi, Chintalapalli and Palamaneru. However, major development took place only after 1970-71.

Sericulture was originally under the control of the Director of Industries and the apex administrator was a Joint Director who dealt with sericulture and other cottage Industries. Sericulture was transferred to the Director of Handlooms and Textiles in 1967. Keeping in view its importance and potential for development, a separate Department of Sericulture was formed by the State Government with effect from 20-04-1981.[17]

The entire state was divided into convenient regions for the purpose of smooth administration by the Dept. of Sericulture. Each region consists of a district or a group of districts. A Deputy Director, an Assistant Director is placed in charge of each region depending on the scale of sericulture. The State Government has set up a Federation of Sericulture and Silk-weavers Co-Operative Societies with Hyderabad as its headquarters. The Director or a person nominated by the Government is its chairperson and a technical expert is appointed as Managing Director. The government nominates the Board of Directors to run the Federation. The Federation has been authorised in a very broad way to carry out any work that would promote Sericulture Development.

Mulberry Cultivation

A phenomenal increase took place in the hectarage under mulberry cultivation from 2,610 to 116.18 thousand hectares between 1970-71 to 1998-99. It is interesting to note that all the area under mulberry is under irrigated conditions. However the Central Sericulture Board has evolved a rainfed variety of mulberry, viz. S_{13} which is under, trial on an experimental basis in some parts of the state like Paderu, Chintalapalle, Araku valley and in Coastal Andhra Pradesh where the rainfall is considerable. The particulars of area under mulberry cultivation in Andhra Pradesh from 1990-91 to 1998-99 is furnished in Table—2.2.

Table—2.2 Area under Mulberry cultivation in Andhra Pradesh

(1990-91 to 1998-99)

Year	*Area under Mulberry (in Thousand hectares)*
1990-91	74.31
1991-92	80.60
1992-93	86.02
1993-94	90.80
1994-95	94.99
1995-96	100.64
1996-97	106.89
1997-98	111.90
1998-99	116.18

Source: Annual Administrative Reports, A.P., Directorate of Sericulture.

It is clear from the Table—2.2 that the area under mulberry cultivation in the state has registered a remarkable growth. Every year there has been an increase in the area under mulberry cultivation. This increase was mainly due to conversion of the land under food crops and a few commercial crops for mulberry cultivation because of its various advantages. The increase in the area under mulberry cultivation has been shown in Graph—2.2. The growth rate is presented in Table—2.3.

Graph—2.2

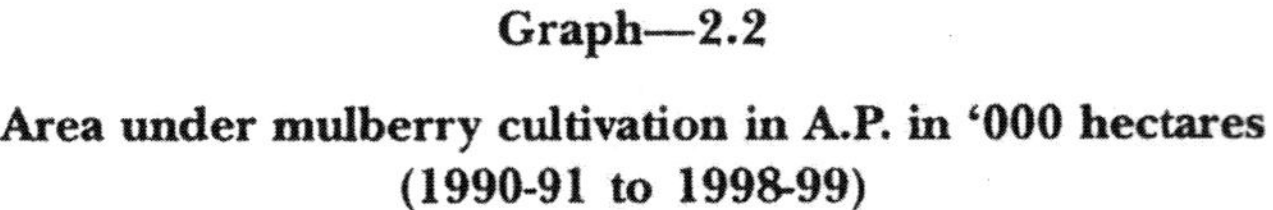

Area under mulberry cultivation in A.P. in '000 hectares (1990-91 to 1998-99)

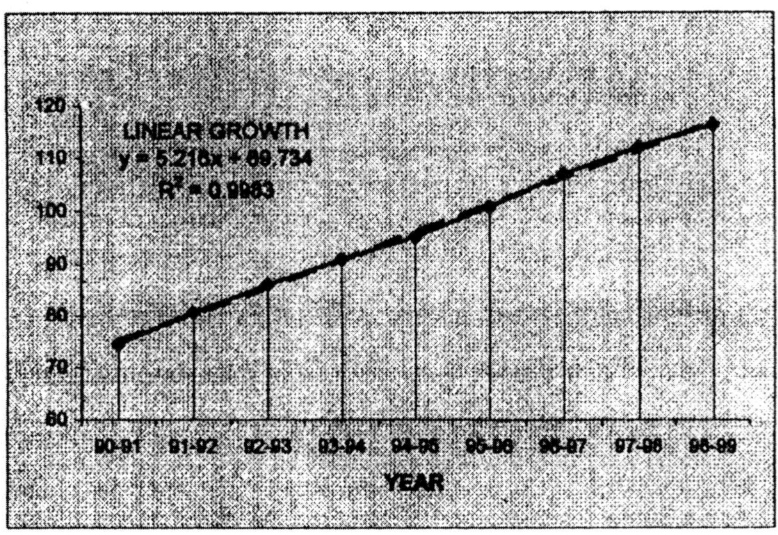

Table—2.3 Growth rate in mulberry cultivation in Andhra Pradesh

Model:		
Y	=	69.73 + 5.216 x
LGR	=	5.4439 per cent
R^2	=	0.9983, F = 4183.4**

** Significant at 1 per cent level

Y = Area under Mulberry cultivation

x = Year

The area under mulberry cultivation has recorded a linear growth of 5.4439 per cent per year. The situation is described in the model shown in Table—2.3. It follows that the growth is significant and if the same trend continues there could be a remarkable area under mulberry cultivation in the coming years.

The concentration of the area under mulberry is mainly in the four districts of Rayalaseema, because of its favourable climatic conditions prevailing in this region for mulberry cultivation. Region wise area under mulberry over a period of nine years from 1990-91 to 1998-99 is shown in Table—2.4.

Table—2.4 Region-wise area under mulberry cultivation in Andhra Pradesh

(1990-91 to 1998-99)

Year	*Rayalaseema*	*Coastal Andhra*	*Telangana*	*Total*
1990-91	57,549 (77.40)	9,072 (12.21)	7,688 (10.34)	74,309 (100.0)
1991-92	60,476 (75.03)	10,460 (12.98)	9,664 (12.06)	80,600 (100.0)
1992-93	63,220 (73.50)	11,816 (13.73)	10,990 (12.77)	86.020 (100.0)
1993-94	65,452 (72.10)	13,082 (14.42)	12,240 (13.46)	90,774 (100.0)
1994-95	67,956 (71.01)	14.633 (15.29)	13,109 (13.7)	95,698 (100.0)
1995-96	71,933 (70.9)	15,519 (15.3)	13,897 (13.72)	1,01,349 (100.0)
1996-97	76,790 (71.3)	16,118 (15.0)	14,698 (13.7)	1,07,606 (100.0)
1997-98	80,324 (71.3)	16,871 (15.0)	15,425 (13.7)	1,12,620 (100.0)
1998-99	84,572 (73.35)	16,902 (14.46)	15,425 (13.19)	1,16,900 (100.0)

Source: Annual Administrative Reports, Directorate of Sericulture, Hyderabad.

Note: Figures in parentheses indicate the percentage to total.

Table—2.4 shows that more than 70 per cent of the land under mulberry cultivation is concentrated in the Rayalaseema region of Andhra Pradesh. The other two regions Coastal and Telangana project a nominal picture. It may also be observed the share of Rayalaseema which was 77.40 per cent in 1990-91 has come down gradually to 73.35 per cent in 1998-99. It implies that the share of the other two regions has increased slowly which may be due to the realisation of the benefits of this crop by the farmers of those regions. However Rayalaseema still forms the major force in the sericulture development of Andhra Pradesh. Statistical analysis of region-wise growth of the area under mulberry cultivation is given in Table—2.5.

Table—2.5 Region-wise growth rate of area under mulberry cultivation

Models:

Rayalaseema

$Y = 51.7866 + 3.804(X)$; LGR = 5.37 per cent

(8.8314)

$R^2 = 0.9176$, $F = 77.99^{**}$

Coastal Andhra

$Y = 8.6975 + 1.0266(X)$; LGR = 7.42 per cent

(12.5769)

$R^2 = 0.9576$, $F = 158.18^{**}$

Telangana

$Y = 7.7948 + 0.9548(X)$; LGR = 7.60 per cent

$R^2 = 0.9476$, $F = 126.6201^{**}$

Total

$Y = 69.5275 + 5.3362\ (X)$; LGR = 5.546 per cent

(75.0127)

$R^2 = 0.9988$ $F = 5626.91^{**}$

Y = Area Under Mulberry Cultivation, X = year.

The area under mulberry cultivation in the three regions of Andhra Pradesh is shown in Graph—2.3. The trend is explained by a linear regression model shown in Table—2.5 and the growth rates are computed. The region-wise as well as the overall growth rates are significant at 1 per cent level.

Cocoon Production

With the increase in area under mulberry cultivation the production of reeling cocoons has also increased substantially. The particulars of production of reeling cocoons in Andhra Pradesh since 1990-91 are given in Table—2.6.

Table—2.6 Cocoon production in Andhra Pradesh

(1990-91 to 1998-99)

Year	*Cocoon Production in A.P Quantity (in thousand tonnes)*
1990-91	32.26
1991-92	27.00
1993-94	34.52
1994-95	24.51
1995-96	22.54
1996-97	22.49
1997-98	24.80
1998-99	30.17

Source: Annual Administrative Reports Directorate of Sericulture, Hyderabad. A.P.

Graph—2.3

Region-wise area under mulberry cultivation in A.P. (in hectares—1990-91 to 1998-99)

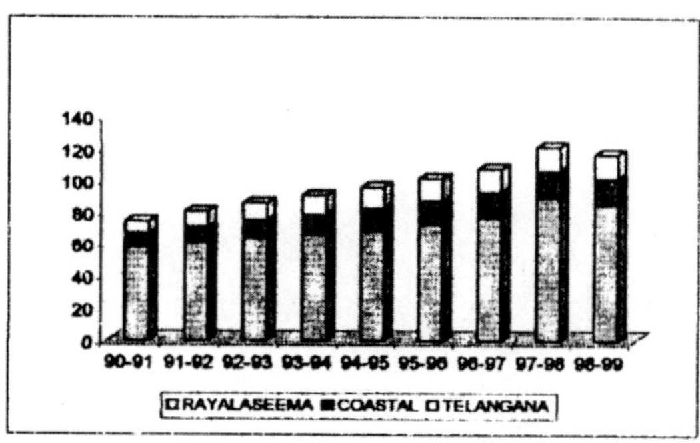

Table—2.6 depicts that the production of reeling cocoons in Andhra Pradesh faced frequent fluctuations during the period from 1990-91 to 1998-99. It is observed that poor quality of layings supplied by the private grainages, lack of timely supply of good quality layings from the government grainages, use of old and outdated rearing appliances and adverse climatic conditions were mainly responsible for the fluctuations in the production of reeling cocoons. This is also shown in Graph—2.4 and the in following model in Table—2.7.

Table—2.7 Growth Rates in Cocoon Production in Andhra Pradesh

Model:
$Y = 0.1411\ X^3 - 1.6644\ X^2 + 3.6992\ X + 29.129$
$R^2 = 0.6989$
Y = Cocoon production
X = Year

It is clear from the above model that the cocoon production is unstable over the study period. However from 95-96 onwards there is a stable growth with a linear growth rate of 7.5 per cent per year. The overall trend shows some sort of a cyclical behaviour described by a mathematical model.

Raw Silk Production

As a result of progress in the field of cocoon production the quantity of raw silk produced also showed an upward trend. The trends in production of raw silk in Andhra Pradesh is shown in the Table—2.8.

Graph—2.4

Cocoon production in Andhra Pradesh
(in '000 tonnes—1990-91 to 1998-99)

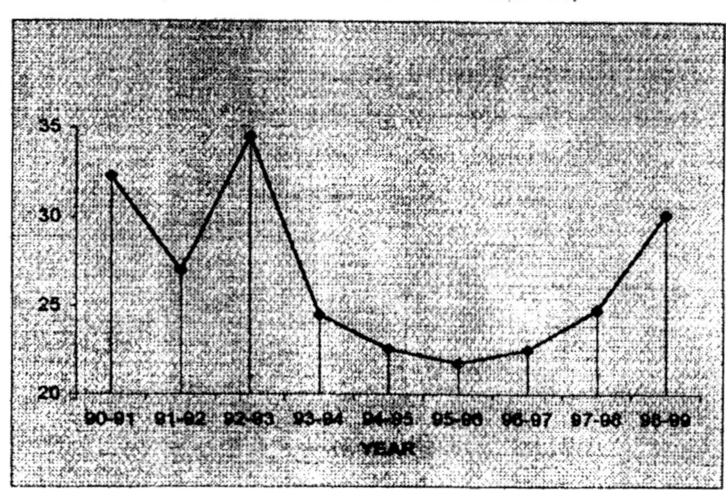

Table—2.8 Trends in raw silk production in Andhra Pradesh

(1990-91 to 1998-99)

Year	*Raw Silk Production (in Thousand tonnes)*
1990-91	3.19
1991-92	2.85
1992-93	3.14
1993-94	2.86
1994-95	2.50
1995-96	2.41
1996-97	2.50
1997-98	2.75
1998-99	3.35

Source: Annual Administrative Reports, Directorate of Sericulture, Hyderabad. A.P.

It is clear from Table—2.8 that the production of raw silk does not steady in Andhra Pradesh. The raw silk production was only 0.08 thousand tonnes in 1980-81 and by the end of 1998-99 it reached 3.35 thousand tonnes. From 1990-91 to 1998-99 it is not stable as shown in Graph—2.5. The production has decreased during 1990-91 to 1995-96 and again started increasing. The trend is described by a polynomial model in time in the Table—2.9.

Table—2.9 Growth rate in raw silk production

Model:

$Y = 0.0219\ X^3 - 0.1526\ X^2 + 3843\ X + 2.8504$

$R^2 = 0.8685$

F = Y = Raw Silk Production

X = Years

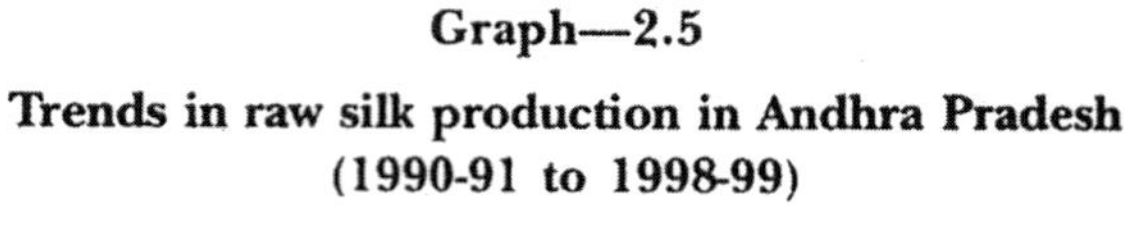

Graph—2.5

Trends in raw silk production in Andhra Pradesh (1990-91 to 1998-99)

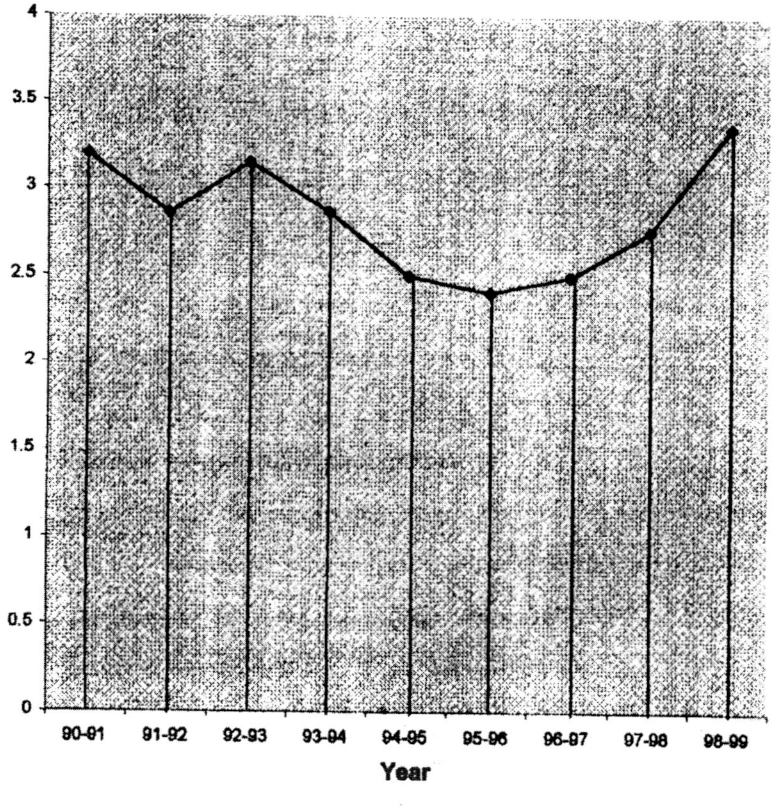

The compound growth rate is computed from 94-95 onwards is 7.4 per cent which is found to be significant.

District-wise Status of Sericulture

Though there is certainly amazing progress in sericulture in Andhra Pradesh, the growth is concentrated only in a few districts of the state. The district-wise particulars of sericulture shown in Table—2.10 presents a clear picture of the status of sericulture during 1998-99.

Table—2.10 District-wise particulars of sericulture in Andhra Pradesh (1998-99)

S. No.	*District*	*Area Under Mulberry Cultivation*	*Cocoon Production in Lakh.Kgs.*
1.	Anantapur	17636	155.698
2.	Kurnool	2528	11.287
3.	Cuddapah	1829	8.700
4.	Chittoor	13773	114.314
5.	Prakasam	746	2.854
6.	Guntur	122	0.383
7.	Nellore	399	0.891
8.	Krishna	436.6	0.586
9.	E. Godavari	445	0.336
10.	W. Godavari	489	1.691
11.	Vizag	471	0.232
12.	Viziayanagaram	193	0.067
13.	Srikakulam	465	0.455
14.	Mahaboobnagar	442	0.446
15.	Ranga Reddy	152	0.056
16.	Nalgonda	137	0.125
17.	Karimnagar	524	0.434
18.	Nizamabad	230	0.164
19.	Adilabad	265	1.127
20.	Warangal	451	0.562
21.	Khammam	302	0.228
22.	Medak	773	1.160
23.	Hyderabad	-	-
	Total	**42,809**	**301.796**

Source: Annual Administrative Reports, Directorate of Sericulture, Hyderabad, Govt. of Andhra Pradesh

It is clear from the Table—2.10 that sericulture activity is highly concentrated in the four Rayalaseema districts of Anantapur, Chittoor, Cuddapah and Kurnool. Among them Anantapur ranks

Graph—2.6

Area under mulberry cultivation—district/region-wise

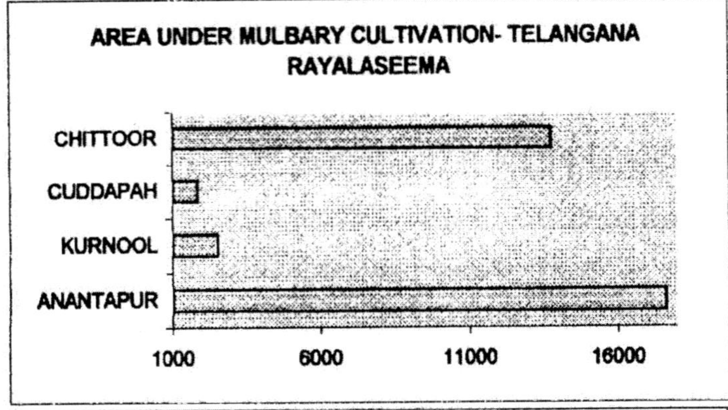

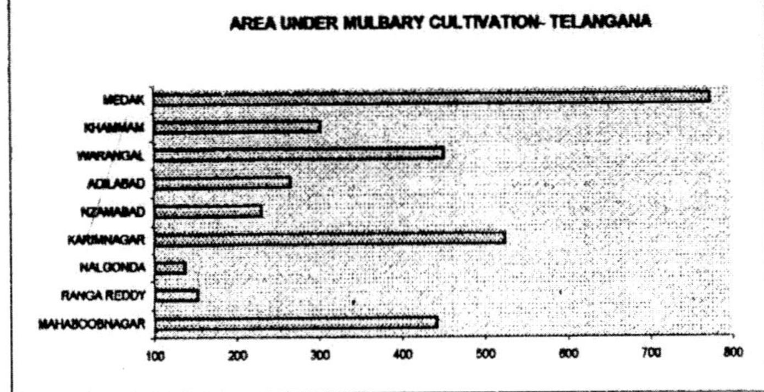

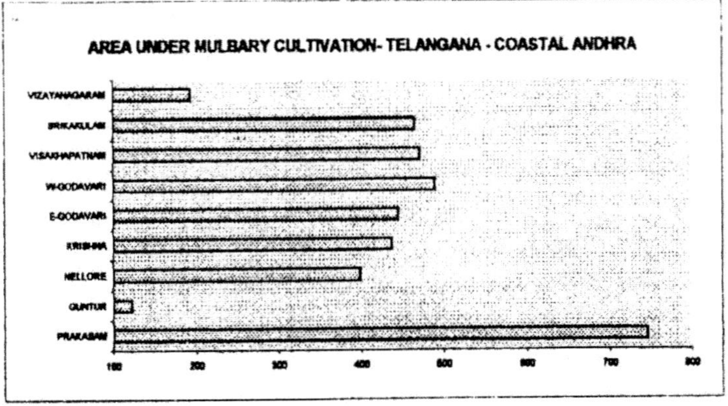

first with 17,636 thousand hectares (41 per cent of the total area), followed by Chittoor with 13,773 hectares. Kurnool and Cuddapah occupy the next places in ranking. Anantapur district occupies the first place in the production of reeling cocoons with 155.698 lakh. kgs which constitute 51.6 per cent of the total cocoon production of Andhra Pradesh.

Thus, Rayalaseema region in the state holds the first place in sericulture activity. This is due to the favourable climatic conditions in these districts and also the rising interest of farmers in this very lucrative activity. This is also shown in Graph—2.6.

Marketing of Reeling Cocoons

The transactions made at the Government cocoon markets and the revenue obtained through the sale of the cocoons are shown in Table—2.11.

Table—2.11 Transactions made in Government cocoon markets in Andhra Pradesh: (1990-91 to 1998-99)

Year	*Quantity of cocoons marketed (in Tonnes)*	*Total value realised (Rs. in Lakhs)*	*Market fee collected (Rs. in Lakhs)*
1990-91	6247	4351.20	87.182
1991-92	5900	6695.00	133.92
1992-93	6870	5834.9	14.678
1993-94	–	–	–
1994-95	5928	5628.141	112.35
1995-96	5567	5741.80	115.70
1996-97	4718	5026.02	100.77
1997-98	5022	5073.10	101.57
1998-99	4972	5436.99	108.97

Source: Annual Administrative Reports, Directorate of Sericulture, Hyderabad. A.P.

Table—2.11 shows that the quantity of cocoons transacted in the Government cocoon markets was low when compared to the total production in the state. Hence there is the need to evaluate the functions of Government cocoon markets and their approach to the sericulturists and the increasing interference of middlemen in the transactions. As the majority of the sericulturists are illiterates and transport facilities from the remote villages are not available, the business of selling cocoons had to be completed in the local unorganised cocoons markets. In addition the risk and strain involved in transporting cocoons to far away government cocoon markets forced them to complete their transactions at the unorganised local markets. After harvesting if the cocoons remain unsold for two or three days worms will develop and come out of the cocoons breaking them open. Then the cocoons become waste and cannot be used.

But some times sericulturists of Andhra Pradesh are seen taking their cocoons to the cocoon markets to the adjacent Karnataka state to get profitable prices for their produce.

The trend in cocoons marketed, market fee collected and the value realised shown an increasing growth rate since 1996-97 with minor variations. The same is depicted in Graph—2.7.

Financial Achievements

The programme-wise financial allocation made during 1998-99 and expenditure incurred up to March, 1999 for sericulture development are indicated below:

Table—2.12 Financial Allocation and Expenditure during 1998-1999.

(Rs. in lakhs)

Sl. No.	*Programme*	*Allocation 1998-99*	*Expenditure 1998-99*
1.	Non-Plan	1929-30	2330.992
2.	Plan	440.00	423.862
	Total	**2369.30**	**2754.852**

Source: Annual Administrative Reports, Directorate of Sericulture, Hyderabad. A.P.

Graph—2.7

Transactions made in Govt. cocoon markets in A.P. (1994-95 to 1998-99)

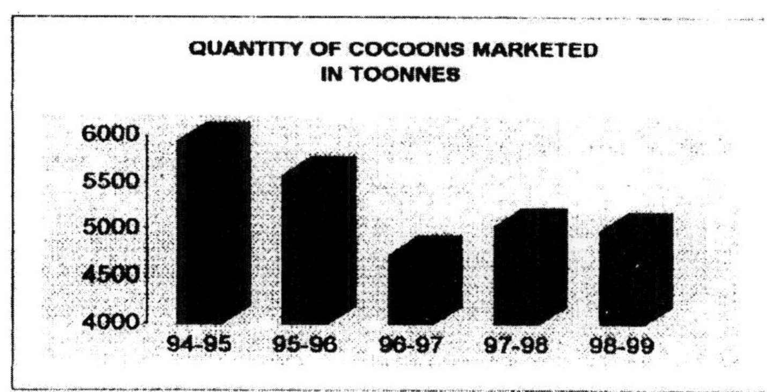

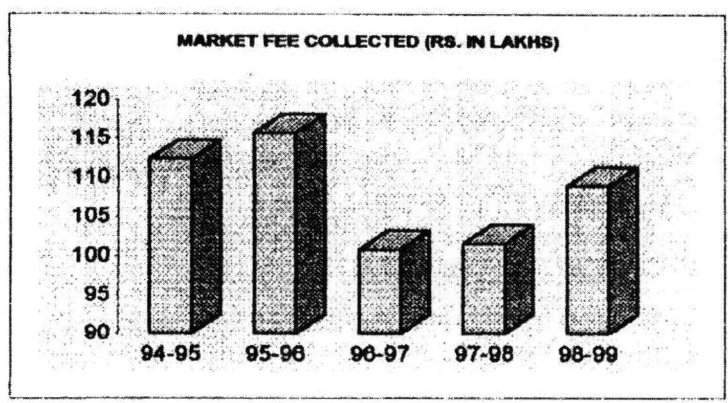

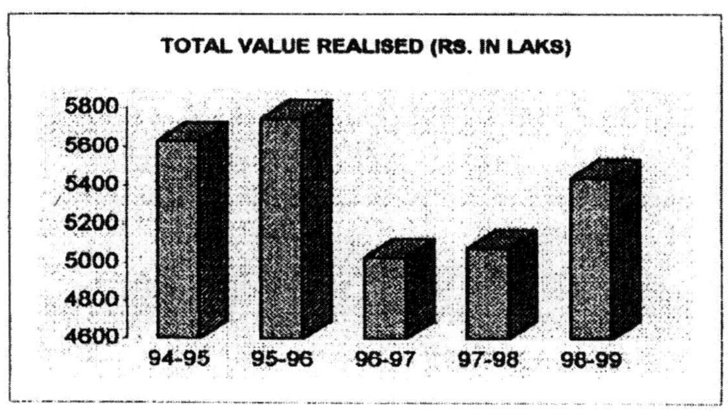

Seed Production

The Sericulture farmers require seed (Disease free silk worm eggs/layings) for production of silk cocoons. These layings are supplied from the CB Grainages. The supply of required quality seed cocoons for the Grainages is ensured through a well organised three tier system of seed multiplication viz., P3, P2, & P1 tiers.

There are two P3 basic seed farms functioning in the state.

(i) Basic Seed farm at Horsley Hills (P3 FR) in Chittoor District.

(ii) Basic Seed farm at Tadakalapalli (P3 LR) in Anantapur District.

In the above two stations, the basic seed stock is maintained from which P2 layings are prepared which in turn are supplied to different P2 farms both Local race (LR) and Foreign race (FR). A total of 29 P2 farms are functioning in the State.

From P2 farms the seed cocoons are sent to P1 grainages where they are processed for preparation of P1 layings. These layings in turn are sent to the seed areas where selected farmers are given the job of converting P1 layings into P1 seed cocoons. The Department also established 29 P1 farms which convert the P1 layings into P1 seed cocoons.

All such P1 seed cocoons of LR & FR are sent to the commercial grainages (CB grainages) where LR & FR cocoons are crossed in order to produce the CB disease free layings (CBDFLs).

Grainages

The seed cocoons which are sent to the commercial grainages are converted into CB layings which are again sold to the farmers at a commercial price. There are 29 commercial grainages functioning in the state under public sector. Government is also encouraging entrepreneurs to establish CB grainages under private sector for supplementing the efforts of the Government in meeting the requirements of seed.

The main objective of these grainages is to supply quality seed to the farmers. It is also heartening to note that the for the first time in the year 1996-97 the Government grainages have been able to make an overall profit of Rs. 15.404 lakhs. For the year 1997-98 the profit in Government grainages is almost doubled. The Profit and loss is arrived at after taking into consideration the variables costs, i.e., staff salaries, wages and working out the depreciation of the building in occupation.

Utmost importance is given for preservation of the basic stock and preparation of different levels of seed upto the CB layings in order to make them totally disease free. At P3 as well as P2 level 100 per cent test checking is taken up in order to avoid diseases such as Pebrine and other deadly diseases. Practices have been standardised at CB grainages also where 10 per cent is test checked for existence of any disease. Hence the disease surveillance system has been improving over a period of time.

Extension

The next important area of the Department is to increase the area under mulberry cultivation consciously. Mulberry cuttings are given from the departmental farms as well as from Karnataka, preferably the high yielding variety of M5, S36, S13, S54, MR2 and V1. Till a few years ago, the cost of transportation of cuttings was borne by the Department/CSB. But now this scheme has been stopped even under NSSP as a result of which the local officers are approaching the District Collectors for some funds for transportation of the improved cuttings. In order to consciously increase the acreage and productivity, the entire state has been divided into Technical Service Centres. There are 162 technical service centres (TSCs) in the state.

The main functions of TSCs are to consolidate the existing mulberry acreage, and to bring additional mulberry acreage. TSc staff also give technical guidance to the farmers under their jurisdiction which is approximately 500 acres in traditional areas and about 250 acres in non-traditional areas. The extension staff identify suitable SC, ST, Small and Marginal farmers to be brought under IRDP, DPAP, ITDA, SC/BC corporation. The staff conduct study tours for farmers as well as women groups to progressive areas of sericulture to show them the improved methods for adoption. Also conduct farmers' meets called "Seri Sadassulu" in different villages to create a forum to create a forum for exchange of ideas among the sericulturists resulting in adoption/transfer of technology.

The Technical Service is looked after by either an Inspector of Sericulture or Asst. Inspector of Sericulture with supporting staff of two Farm Foremen and four operators.

Marketing

Another very important major area has been opening up of Cocoon Markets in 22 places of which 8 cocoon markets are regular cocoon markets while the rest are notified cocoon markets. These cocoon markets were opened up for the first time in Andhra Pradesh in 1981. Till then all the farmers were going to Karnataka Cocoon Markets i.e., Ramnagar, Siddalagattla for selling their cocoons or to middlemen who used to exploit the sericulturists. It is interesting to note that after the introduction of cocoon markets the main cocoon markets are now transacting 5900 MTs and there has been an extensive increase in the last 7 years from 3972 MTs to 5900 MTs. Market fee @ 1% from the reeler and 1% from the farmer is collected. There has been substantial increase in the market arrivals and market fee in the cocoon markets steadily. Improvements were made to the existing cocoon markets, and greater emphasis has been given on cocoon testing. 10% of lots are compulsorily checked for quality as well as disease surveillance. The department has been further improving these practices to increase test checking to 30% to 40% and also to keep the farmers informed of the quality of their cocoons before the product is put to auction. This will go a long way in improving the productivity of the rearers produce for which the reeler will give a better price in future. Input sales centres are also run by 'Serifed' in the cocoon markets where disinfectants and other sericulture equipment required by rearers are supplied at reasonable prices. The notified markets are the Govt. Reeling units taken up in non-traditional area in order to enable the rearers to sell their cocoons at the notified markets since purchase and sale of cocoon is regulated by the A.P. Seed and Cocoon Control Act. 1956.

Priority is given in cocoon markets to women farmers at the time of auction as well as payment. Rest houses are also provided for women in all the major cocoon markets. These measures help women farmers to have access to the resources. Each major market has an auditorium with facilities like audio visual aids, seating arrangements etc., for showing the films on improved technologies.

Post Cocoon Sector

A very important area which has been engaging the attention of the Department has been the post cocoon i.e., the reeling, twisting and weaving areas. Government was running 54 reeling clusters till recently employing its own staff who were trained in these processes. Because of continuous losses incurred by running these units, most of them have been closed with an exception of 16 reeling clusters which are still being run utilising only a marginal fraction of their existing capacity. There has been a lot of negotiation with private persons on leasing out/sale of these units to them. A number of private parties have come forward and have shown enthusiasm in running these units. Under the World Bank aided NSP consciously 10 reeling clusters have been taken up in order to repair and modernise the existing machinery and to lease them out to in certain private parties. The Department has established 14 Non-farm TSCs for the development of post cocoon sector in the state. The achievements made in sericulture sector as a result of continuous support from the Government of Andhra Pradesh is shown in Table—2.13.

Table—2.13 The achievements made during 1999-2000 and 2000-01 (upto June)

Sl. No.	*Item*	*1999-2000*	*2000-01 (Upto June'00)*
1	2	3	4
1.	Employment generation (Lakh persons)	5.58	5.58
2.	Area under mulberry cultivation (Cumulative in acres)	1,11,602	1,11,602
3.	CBDfls production (In Lakh nos.)	2,17,852	30,689
4.	Cocoon production (In Mts.)	34,193	8,007
5.	Raw Silk production (In Mts.).	3,757	879
6.	Sericulture farmers (In lakh no.)	1,07,000	1,07,000
7.	Tasar food plantation available for rearing (In acres).	21,000	21,000
8.	Tasar Dfls brushed (In Lakh Nos.)	3.32	0.26

(Table Contd...)

1	2	3	4
9.	Tasar Cocoon production(In Lakh Nos.)	16.95	Crops under progress
10.	Tasar Cocoon production (In Lakh Nos.)	3,000	3,000
11.	Silk Weavers (under Co-operative fold)	30,000	30,000
12.	Silk Co-op societies (In Nos.)	324	324

Source: Annual Administrative Report, Directorate of Sericulture, Hyderabad. A.P.

Unit Cost at Present

The Government has increased the amount of financial assistance for cultivating mulberry and for the construction of rearing shed during the year 1999-2000. The amount has been raised from Rs. 19,880 to Rs. 67,000. The breakup of amount is as follows:

1.	Mulberry cultivation	:	Rs. 9,000/-
2.	Silkworm Rearing equipment	:	Rs. 8,000/-
3.	Shed cost (Pucca & Rcc)	:	Rs. 58,000/-
			Rs. 67,000

Programmes and Projects in Andhra Pradesh

I. Indo-Swiss project

A project with the financial assistance of Switzerland Government through the Swiss development co-operation, was started in 1987-88 in Andhra Pradesh with an objective of improving the status of the small and marginal farmers engaged in sericulture. This project has completed Phase-I and Phase-II. Now at present the III phase of the project has been started during the year 1998. The project period is 1998-2002.

Schemes are proposed for implementation in Andhra Pradesh during the first year project and the details are given below.

(a) Organisation of Productivity Clubs in on Farm Sector

The scheme is proposed to organise productivity clubs in order to impart technical and managerial knowledge through participatory approach and to encourage the sericulturists to move towards adoption of new technologies for increasing productivity and also income levels for sustenance of sericulture. An amount of Rs. 8.75 Lakhs is allotted to organise (50) productivity clubs in Anantapur, Chittoor, Krishna and Medak districts of the state during the first year of the project.

The Schedule Castes (S.C) corporation and Backward Caste (B.C) corporation agreed to sanction 20 per cent of margin money to the beneficiaries. The S.C corporation has allotted 30 per cent of the total money sanctioned to women sericulturists to take up sericulture activity.

(b) Training of Bivoltine Seed Rearers

The scheme is proposed to train bivoltine seed rearers couple in better management skills is traditional bivoltine seed areas of Karnataka and to increase the production of quality of bivollene seed cocoons. An amount of Rs. 6.12 lakhs is allocated to implement this component in Anantapur, Chittoor, Visakhapatnam and Ranga Reddy districts during 1998-99.

(c) Computerised Mis

This scheme is proposed for development of fast communication system in sericulture industry to monitor seed production programme. Disease of surveys and surveillance and passing of extension message and day to day cocoon and silk market trends for taking quick decision by concerned authority. The main objective of this scheme is easy flow of information for taking quick/ correct decisions and assess cocoon and silk yarn prices besides fair and easy cocoon transaction in cocoon markets. An amount of Rs. 9.45 Lakhs is allotted to implement this component during 1998-99.

The project SERI-2000 is proposed to implementation in Anantapur, Chittoor, Medak, Krishna, Ranga Reddy/ Vizayanagaram districts of Andhra Pradesh with a total cost of Rs. 24.32 Lakhs.

II. Extension Activities

Study tours have been organised for farmers/reelers/weavers especially from non-traditional areas to provide opportunity to interact and observe the nature of various types of sericultural activities among the farmer/reelers and weavers in the traditional areas.

(a) On-farm Sector

A credit of Rs. 512.64 Lakhs has been sanctioned and distributed during 1998-99 under on-farm sector. An additional area of 10574 acres has been brought under mulberry against the target of 10,000 acres during 1998-99. 30,179 tonnes of reeling cocoons have been produced by the rearers against the target 25,000 tonnes. The estimated raw silk production is 3,335 tonnes based on cocoon production.

(b) Non-farm Sector

A credit of Rs. 86.06 Lakhs has been sanctioned for establishment of 163 units under reeling sector during the year 1998-99.

III. Sericulture Development Fund (S.D.F)

During the year 1998-99 an amount of Rs.50.00 lakhs was released under S.D.F towards various programmes, out of which a sum of Rs.49.80 lakhs was incurred.

SECTION-III

Women in Sericulture

Employment opportunities for women are also high in sericulture Industry. Various operations in the production of silk beneficially engage women. Sericulture, because of its unique nature of work, proves to be an ideal activity for women who can work in addition to their regular tasks of taking care of the family. Its operation do not require hard labour. Almost all the sericulture activities, except such tasks digging, ploughing and carrying heavy loads, which are strenuous can be carried out by women independently. Silk-worms being delicate have to be handled with proper care. Thus the entire process of rearing needs expertise, high skill and patience. Women possess these qualities to an eminent degree and therefore are more suitable than men. It is worked out that about 2,575 women work days comprising about 60 per cent are generated per annum out of a total of about 4,225 work days in all the activities in sericulture per hectare of irrigated mulberry. Thus sericulture provides scope for the direct involvement of women in the process of production and decision making for improving their economic conditions and for giving them greater recognition and status in the family and society. Under the National Sericulture Project, the action plan on women envisages group-formation, special training programmes for women, allotment of land in the names of the women, special credit schemes for women etc. All these programmes are under implementation for raising the active participation of women in sericulture.

Women Development Programme

During the year 1998-99 an amount of R.500 lakhs has been sanctioned towards the scheme "one time assistance to women group" for (5) women groups and training programme to 833 women.

Women

Women contribute 60% work force in Sericulture. Like nurturing family, their involvement in sericulture is also highly significant and needs a special mention. National Sericulture Project recognised their achievements and the year 1994 was declared as 'Year of Women in Sericulture'.

Central Silk Board, State Sericulture Departments and various non-governmental agencies made a concerted effort to improve access to resources, to enhance managerial and entrepreneurial autonomy and to acquire better technology and skills during the last eight years. Time bound action plans were chalked out and task forces at Central and State level monitored the achievements year to year which were oriented towards:

1. Emphasizing productive role of women in sericulture through creation of better training facilities, extension mechanisms, women friendly infrastructural facilities and improving women's access to credit.
2. Stimulating formation of women with financial support for taking up sericulture related income generating activities.

3. Involving non-governmental organisations (NGOs) for upliftment of women, Scheduled Castes(SCs), Scheduled Tribes(STs) and economically weaker sections.
4. Sensitizing Staff, farmers and entrepreneurs to gender dimensions.
5. Promoting smokeless chulhas in reeling, minimizing health hazards and developing women friendly technologies.
6. Creating substantial job opportunities for women.

The following scheme is exclusively implemented under Annual Plan schemes. In rest of the schemes it is proposed to cover 33% as per Govt. orders.

Name of the scheme	*Scheme/Objective*
Women Development Programmes	1. Formation of women groups to provide financial assistance to the organised women groups for ensuring mutual support and to enhance their status in the household, community in terms of decision making and control over resources and benefit derived from such sources.
	2. Training to women in new technology to improve their technical knowledge and to improve the productivity

Conclusion

Today sericulture has developed to a status of a well knit agro-based, labour intensive cottage industry in the world. 'Silk' is the queen of textiles and it occupies a prestigious place among all fibres. Sericulture in India has a very long history. A few years ago, sericulture has been considered a subsidiary occupation of poor farmers. But now with the continuous support of the Government of India it has achieved the position of main occupation in certain parts of our country. Andhra Pradesh is the state next to Karnataka in production of mulberry raw silk. Sericulture has gained momentum during the last two decades in Andhra Pradesh and made remarkable progress. The Government of Andhra Pradesh through the implementation of a variety of programmes encouraging farmers to take-up this occupation. Especially women are also given special training, assistance and encouragement in this activity.

REFERENCES

1. Sanjay Sinha, *The Development of Indian Silk*, Oxford and IBH Publishing Co. Pvt. Ltd, New Delhi, p. 4. 1986.
2. S.R. Charley, *Culture and Sericulture*, Academic Press, London, 1982, p. 69.
3. Sanjay Sinha, *The Development of Indian Silk*, Op. cit., p. 5.
4. Ibid, p. 7.
5. S. Muniraju, "*Sericulture a Tool for Rural Development*", Souvenir on International Congress on Tropical Sericulture Practices, Feb, 1988, SWISS Development Corporation, New Delhi and Central Silk Board, pp. 3-5.
6. Dr. D.V. Ramana, *Economics of Sericulture and Silk Industry in India*, Deep & Deep Publications, New Delhi, 1987, p. 20.
7. Dr. Manjeet, S. Jolly, "*Appropriate Sericulture Techniques, International Centre for Training and Research*, Mysore, 1987, p. 106.
8. Mrs. Prabha Sekhar and C. Ravi Kumar "*Role of Women in Indian Sericulture*". Proceedings of the International Congress on Tropical Sericulture practices. Op. cit, pp. 105-108.
9. D.L. Narayana, *Economics of Sericulture in Rayalaseema*, Op. cit., p. 65.
10. K.V. Benchamin and Manjeet Jolly, "*Employment and Income Generation in the Rural Areas Through Sericulture, Indian Silk*", Vol. XXVI. No. 2, June 1987, p. 9.
11. D.V. Ramana, *Economics of Sericulture and Silk Industry in India*, Op. cit, p. 37.
12. Venkata Narasaiah, *Sericulture in India*, Ashish Publishing House, New Delhi, 1992, pp. 17-19.
13. A.R.S. Gopalachar, *Three Decades of Sericulture Progress*, Central Silk Board, Bangalore, 1978, p. 3.
14. C. Ravikumar and Pratha Sekhar, "*Contribution of Sericulture for Rural Development in India*", Proceedings of the International Congress on Tropical Sericulture Practices, Op. cit, pp. 77-80.
15. Andhra Pradesh State Gazetteer, Govt. of India, Hand book. p. 4.
16. "*New Horizons for Sericulture in Andhra Pradesh*", Dept. of Textiles and Handlooms, 1976, p. 6.
17. Smt. Asha Murthy, "*Sericulture in Andhra Pradesh*", "Souvenir on International Congress on Tropical Sericulture Practices, February, 1988.

3

Progress of Sericulture in Rayalaseema Region

As already mentioned in the earlier chapters, sericulture has been making rapid strides of progress in Andhra Pradesh state, particularly in Rayalaseema Region. Anantapur and Chittoor districts in the state have the unique distinction of producing mulberry silk and also have sericulture deeply rooted in almost all of their blocks. In Rayalaseema Region sericulture is practised under irrigated conditions. Inspite of severe drought and low rainfall conditions, mulberry cultivation in this region has increased enormously during the last 15 years. As mulberry is drought resistant, sericulture has become the most promising activity to the farmers in these four districts.

In this chapter an attempt is made to analyse in detail about sericulture development in the districts namely Anantapur, Kurnool, Cuddapah and Chittoor. It is felt that a brief discussion of the economy, growth and present status of sericulture in these districts is essential for the purpose of full length review. Therefore the present chapter is divided into two sections. In the first section, the progress and the status of sericulture in the sample districts is presented. In the second section the socio-economic status of the respondents is discussed.

SECTION—I

Development of Sericulture in Rayalaseema Region

Climatic conditions prevailing in this region are more favourable for the development of mulberry cultivation and silk worm rearing. Among the four districts Anantapur and Chittoor are nearer to Karnataka state. Karnataka being the premier state, has rich heritage of sericulture. The other factor that govern the localisation of sericulture in these districts is severe drought conditions. While all other agricultural crops wither away, mulberry crop survives and yields atleast two crops out of five crops. In addition to the above factor, one more important factor is the availability of financial assistance from state and central governments, with a view to improve drought areas and to benefit small and marginal farmers in the above districts.

Out of 42,809 hectares of total area under mulberry cultivation in 1998-99, 35,766 (i.e., 83.55%) is in Rayalaseema Region. Out of 301.796 lakh kgs. of cocoons produced in 1998-99, 2,89,999 lakh kgs. (i.e. 96%) was from Rayalaseema districts.

The progress of sericulture in the four districts is presented in the following pages. Though the region is known for frequent droughts and famines, it is rich in terms of the development of sericulture.

Anantapur District

The Anantapur district was formed in the year 1882 separating it from the then, Bellary district. The district lies between 13° 4'-15° 15' North latitudes and 76° 51'-78° 30' east longitudes. It is the Southern most district of the Rayalaseema Region. Anantapur district is bounded by Cuddapah, Kurnool and Chittoor districts on the east, north, south respectively and by the Karnataka state on the west.[1] The district has been divided into 63 revenue mandals under three Revenue Divisions viz. Anantapur, Dharmavaram and Penukonda.

As per 1991 census, the total population of the district is 31,83,814 of which 24,35,761 (77 per cent) live in rural areas. The density of population is 166 per sq.km. The working force forms 43 per cent of which 39 per cent is in the agriculture sector.[2]

The geographical conditions of the district which is in the middle of the peninsula, render it as the driest part of the state and hence, agricultural conditions are more often than not precarious. Mansoons evade this part due to its unfortunate location. The normal rainfall in the district is 544mm the lowest in comparison with that of the other Rayalaseema districts and other parts of Andhra Pradesh.

The soils in Anantapur district are predominantly red (76.5 per cent) and there are about 23.5 per cent of black soils. Agriculture is the main occupation in the district. The total geographical area of the district is 19.13 lakh hectares, of which the normal cultivated area accounts for 9.66 lakh hectares. The district occupies the second lowest position in Andhra Pradesh with regard to surface irrigation facilities and hence the farmers have to depend more and more on groundwater resources which are being exploited through dug wells and bore wells. The main crops grown in the district are paddy, wheat, Jowar, Ragi, pulses, Groundnut, Mulberry and other millets. Paddy and Jowar are the major food crops whereas groundnut and mulberry are grown as important commercial crops. There has been a slow transformation from traditional crops to non-traditional crops in the district. Although a number of commercial crops are under cultivation in the district, mulberry seems to dominate over many others, both in terms of area and returns. Sericulture has thus attracted a large number of farmers and it has occupied a significant place in the agricultural economy of the district.

Sericulture, as already mentioned occupies the first place in sericulture development in the state as mulberry is fully concentrated in the district. The district is widely known for its 'Dharmavaram silk sarees'. The major factors responsible for the concentration of sericulture in the district are its favourable climatic conditions conducive to silk worm rearing and cocoon production.

Talamarla, a village of the erstwhile Kadiri Taluk, first appeared in the year 1923-24 on the sericulture map of Andhra Pradesh. Again in 1946, Sri Venkatappa, a resident of Veebhuthi palli, now belonging to 'Lepakshi Mandal' started cultivating mulberry in an area of 2.00 hectares. However cultivation of mulberry did not take much headway for another two and half decades due to lack of knowledge and Government assistance. It gained momentum only after the implementation of the Drought prone Areas programme in the district in 1975.

There were only 3 , 560 mulberry growers in the district at that time. Slowly, with the gradual rise in the prices of cocoons and intensives provided to farmers for plantation, construction of rearing sheds etc, created ideal conditions for the astonishing progress of sericulture in the district. Now sericulture is being practised in almost all the 63 manuals of the district and account for nearly 30 per cent of the total area under mulberry cultivation.

With the encouragement given by the state government sericulture in Anantapur district has been progressing to reach commendable heights. Mulberry cultivation and silkworm rearing has become a boon and transformed the life styles of several farmers especially the small and marginal farmers. By 1998-99 mulberry was grown in 42,789 hectares and the cocoon production was 155.69 lakh kgs.

Kurnool District

This district derives its name from its chief town Kurnool. Kurnool district lies between the northern latitudes of 14° 54′ and 16° 11′ and eastern longitudes of 76° 58′ and 78° 25′. The altitude of the district varies from 100ft, above the mean sea level. The district is bounded on the north by Tungabadra and Krishna rivers as well as Mahaboobnagar district, on the south by Cuddapah and Anantapur districts, on the west by Karnataka state and on the east by Prakasam district. The area of the district is 7,658 sq.km. covered by 29,73,024 population as per 1991 census with a density of 168 persons per sq.km. At present Kurnool district comprises of three Revenue Divisions and 54 Revenue Mandals.[3]

Major part of the district consists of black cotton soils, and the south eastern parts are predominantly poor red soils. The District's normal rainfall is 630 mm. The net area sown is 9.07 lakh hectares forming 52 per cent to the total geographical area. The major food crops in the district are rice, jowar and bajra. Groundnut, tobacco cotton and mulberry are also grown. The district consists of 13,40,980 working population out of which women from 5,10,807 as per 1991 census.[4]

Sericulture is better suited for drought prone areas. Kurnool district is one among the frequently drought affected districts of Rayalaseema and sericulture suitably finds its place in the district. Sericulture was first introduced in the district during 1975-76 in Bapananthapuram village of Atmakur Mandal. The area under mulberry was gradually increased over the years to 10,000 acres covering almost all mandals in the district upto 1990 and the area stood at all time high in 1990. But in the subsequent years the net area got reduced because of large scale uprootings by existing farmers due to losses suffered by them on account of steep fall in cocoon price. The out break of deadly pebrine disease in 1991-92, scanty and erratic rains condition and continuous dry spell also major factors for uprooting . However due to its lucrative income the area under mulberry is developed in the district very significantly. Both L.R and S.R seed farms and Seed Area in the district is well developed. Now the district is self sufficient and even supplying seed cocoon to neighbouring districts. As for non-farm sector in sericulture in the district, one 6 basin multiend silk reeling unit, one 6 basin silk reeling unit and 40 country charkas and a complex of 100 twin charkas are established in private sector. As many as 3.000 silk looms are functioning in Adoni area. During the year 1998-99 the area under mulberry cultivation was 8,754 hectares and the cocoon production was 11.28 lakh kgs.

Cuddapah District

This district was first formed in the early nineteenth century during the British rule. Geographically, Cuddapah district is bounded by Kurnool district on the north side, Chittoor on the south side, Nellore on the east side and Anantapur on the west side i.e., the area is located between the 79° 29′ and 79° 55′ eastern and 13°-43′ and 15°-14′ Northern latitudes. The geographical area is 15,359 sq.kms. covered by three Revenue Divisions and 50 Revenue mandals. The total population of the district is 22.66 lakhs of which 17.23 lakhs (76 per cent) being rural and 5.43 lakhs (24 per cent) being urban. The density of population is 147/sq.km.[5]

The district consists of 8,23,654 working population out of which 6,08,782 are engaged in agriculture as cultivators and agricultural labourers. The district gets normal rainfall of 692.2 mm.[6] The major food crops in the district are Rice, Jowar, Bajra and Ragi. Chillies, Turmeric, Sugarcane, Groundnut and Mulberry are also grown. Cuddapah district occupies fourth place in the sericulture map of Andhra Pradesh.

In Cuddapah district mulberry cultivation was started in an extent of few hundred acres during 1970 and at present it has goneup to 8,178 hectares during 1998-99. The cocoons produced during 1998-99 are 8.70 lakh kgs. There were 7,800 farmers depending on sericulture. The area under mulberry cultivation is also expected to grow rapidly in due course. Rayachoti, Lakkireddypalli and Rajampet are some of the places where sericulture has some progress in this district.

Chittoor District

Chittoor district was constituted in 1911. The district is bounded on the North by Anantapur and Cuddapah districts, in the east by Nellore district and Chengalpattu district of Tamilnadu, on the South by North Arcot district of Tamilnadu and on the west by Tamilnadu and Karnataka states. The district covers an extent of 15.152 sq.kms. It is divided into three Revenue Divisions viz., Chittoor, Tirupati and Madanapalle. It is situated between 12°-37 to 14°-8′ of Northern latitude and 78°-33′ to 79°-55′ of the eastern longitude.[7]

The climate of the district is dry and healthy. The district has the benefit of receiving rainfall during both the South West and North East monsoon periods. The normal rainfall of the District for the South West monsoon period is 380.4 mms, and that of North-East monsoon period is 410.5mm. The major portion of the district is covered by red soils with portions of alluvial soil in Chittoor and Bangarupalem erstwhile taluks. The total geographical area is 37,03,537 acres out of which the net area sown is 12,17,284 acres. The density of population is 215 per sq.km. The working population consists of 14.02 lakhs as per 1991 census. The Principle crops are Paddy, Seasamom, Groundnut, Sugarcane, Cotton and Mulberry.[8]

Chittoor district ranks second in area and Cocoon production in the state. Sericulturists adopted both kanva$_2$ and local varieties of mulberry growing. As a result the area under mulberry cultivation has increased from 2,290.5 hectares in 1979 -80 to 9,204,18 hectares in 1988-89 since the inception of Drought from areas programme.[9] The raw silk production also increased from 8.30 lakh kgs. in 1980-81 to 63.020 lakh kgs. in 1988-89.

A silk worm seed unit was established at Horsely hills in 1980-81 with the help of District Rural Development Agency. This unit located at an altitude of 1,424 m, above mean sea level was started for the purpose of supplying cross breed layings for the farmers in different districts. For this purpose, this unit obtained P_3 silk cocoon seed from the breeds stock of CSTRI, Mysore and after rearing the required quantity of P_2 seed is produced and supplied to the seed farms in the state.[10]

An Indo-Japanese venture for the production of bivoltine and multi voltine eggs has been started at Ramasamudram in Punganur Taluk. The capacity of this unit is about 1.20 lakh boxes per annum. This project is first of its kind in the country started producing in 1989. During the year 1998-99 the area under mulberry cultivation was 25, 251 hectares and the quantity of cocoons produced was 1,14,32 lakh kgs.

In the following pages the progress of sericulture in the four Rayalaseema district has been presented. Table—3.1 depicts a clear picture of the growth of area under mulberry cultivation since 1990-91 to 1998-99.

Table—3.1 Area under mulberry cultivation in Rayalaseema region (from 1990-91 to 1998-99)

(in hectares)

Year	*Anantapur*	*Chittoor*	*Kurnool*	*Cuddapah*	*Total*
1990-91	29,861	15,198	6,348	6,141	57,548
1991-92	31,167	16,221	6,620	6,467	60,475
1992-93	32,314	17,329	6,835	6,732	63,210
1993-94	33,190	18,107	7,161	6,983	65,441
1994-95	34,605	18,971	7,468	7,306	68,350
1995-96	36,135	20,550	7993	7,650	72,328
1996-97	38,492	22,275	8,536	7,883	77,186
1997-98	40,232	23,557	8,754	8,178	80,721
1998-99	42,789	25,251	8,754	8,178	84,972
CGR	4.4978	6.5	4.56	3.83	4.995

Source: Annual Administrative Reports Directorate of Sericulture, Hyderabad. A.P.

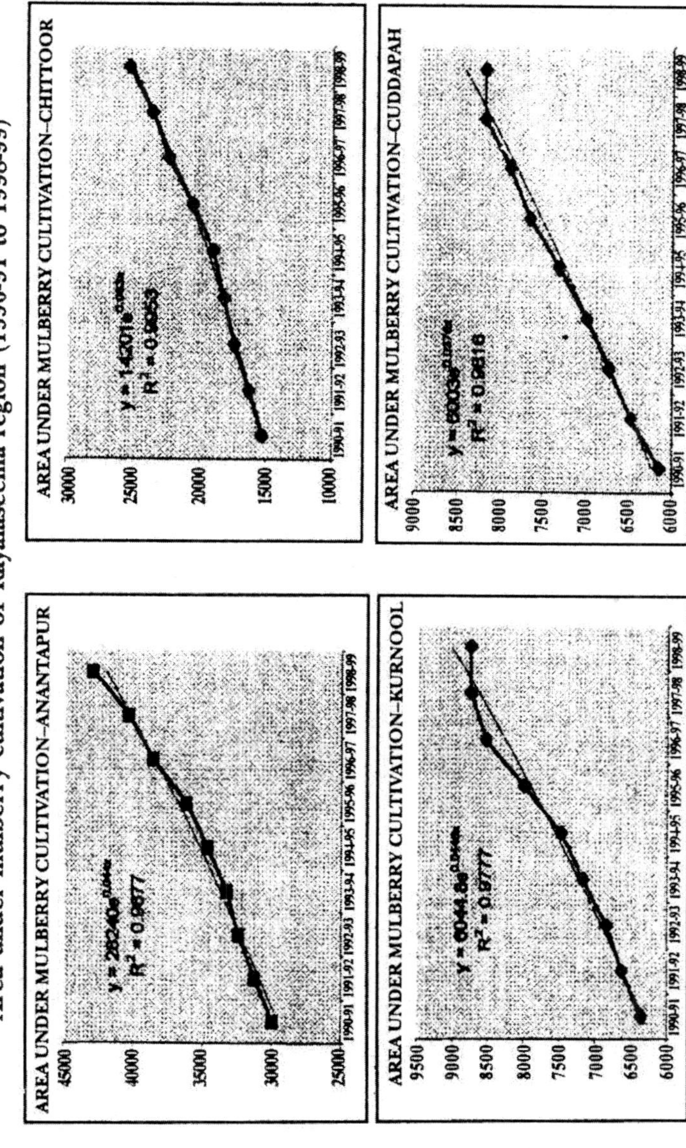

Graph—3.1

Area under mulberry cultivation of Rayalaseema region (1990-91 to 1998-99)

It is clear from the Table—3.1 that the area under mulberry cultivation in Rayalaseema Region has increased from 57,548 hectares (1990-91) to 84,972 hectares (1998-99) during the last nine years, Its can be observed from the table that Anantapur and Chittoor districts are ranking first and second in order in terms of area under mulberry cultivation. There has been a significant increase in the mulberry acreage in these two districts. This increase is more clearly depicted in the Graph—3.1. The overall growth rate in Rayalaseema Region during 1990-91 to 1998-99 was 4.995. In Anantapur it was 4.4978 and in Chittoor it was 6.5 Out of four Rayalaseema districts Chittoor showed 6.5 per cent growth rate during the last decade, which was even higher than the Region's overall growth rate. Cuddapah district noticed only 3.83 per cent growth rate.

Cocoon Production

The production of reeling cocoons in the four Rayalaseema districts is shown in Table—3.2. The reeling cocoon production in Anantapur and Chittoor districts is steadily rising along with the rise in the area under mulberry cultivation.

Table—3.2 Cocoons produced in Rayalaseema Region since 1990-91 to 1998-99

(in Lakh. Kgs)

Year	*District*			
	Anantapur	*Chittoor*	*Kurnool*	*Cuddapah*
1990-91	147.37	85.62	26.03	24.76
1991-92	17.13	84.51	16.67	12.06
1992-93	179.00	95.68	14.9	13.93
1993-94	114.69	80.79	10.06	9.65
1994-95	101.49	84.40	8.82	6.88
1995-96	96.22	85.47	7.84	5.91
1996-97	106.74	84.16	11.06	7.63
1997-98	122.92	97.64	9.25	6.56
1998-99	155.69	114.31	11.28	8.70
CGR	-1.40	+2.34	-9.45	-12.05
Total				**-1.12**

Source: Annual Administrative Reports, Directorate of Sericulture, Hyderabad. A.P.

It is clear from the Table—3.2 that there has been a declining trend in the compound growth rate of cocoon production in Rayalaseema Region (i.e.1.12 per cent). Though there is a raising trend in all the four districts with some fluctuations during 1993-94 to 1996-97, the sample districts noticed a decline in the growth rate during the period from 1990-91 to 1998-99. This may be due to the inferior quality of Cbdfls reared and diseases to silkworms. The trends in cocoon production are shown in Graph—3.2. The production dfls is shown in Table—3.3.

Production of Disease Free Layings

Table—3.3 Production of disease free layings (dfts) since 1990-91 to 1998-99

(in lakh Nos.)

Year	*District*			
	Anantapur	*Chittoor*	*Kurnool*	*Cuddapah*
1990-91	108.51	71.285	16.55	19.51
1991-92	173.79	55.91	26.82	2.73
1992-93	177.27	103.52	26.36	24.00
1993-94	81.50	20.71	21.86	13.8
1994-95	68.514	37.011	11.410	9.793
1995-96	97.771	56.218	12.820	9.763
1996-97	81.139	79.898	11.920	8.671
1997-98	106.819	88.371	12.118	5.25
1998-99	92.637	57.725	10.765	6.19
CGR	-5.64	-1.70	-10.07	-16.88
Total				**-4.54**

Source: Annual Administrative reports, Directorate for sericulture, Hyderabad. A.P.

Graph—3.2

Cocoons produced in Rayalaseema region since (in lakh kgs- 1990-91 to 1998-99)

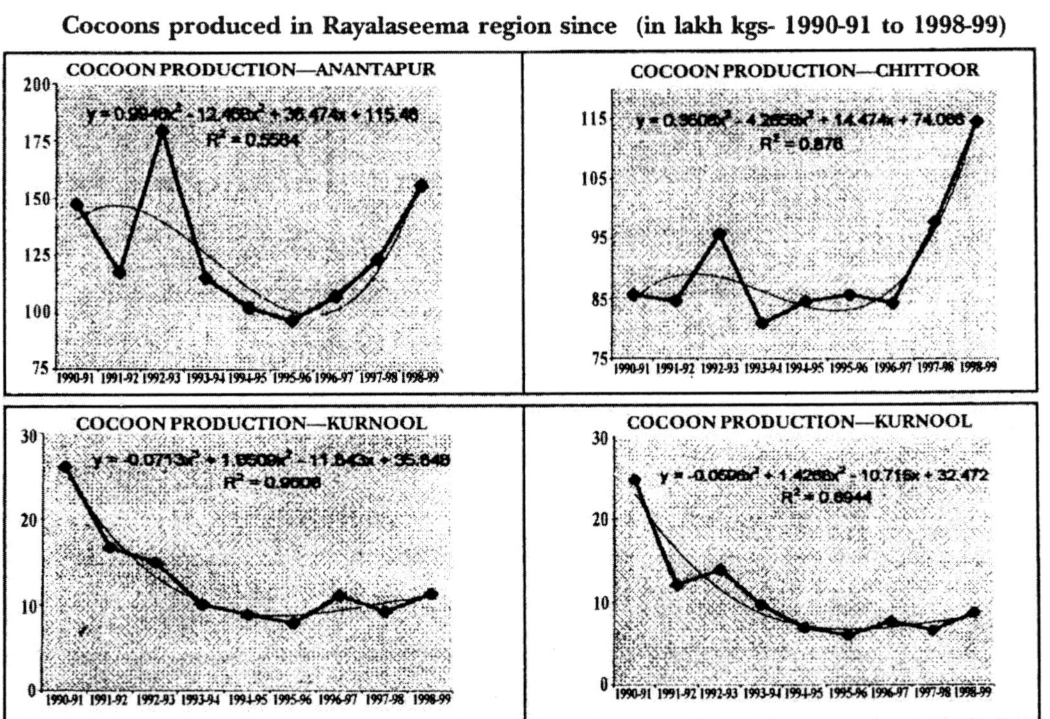

It is seen from the Table—3.3, that as the hectarage under mulberry cultivation increased year after year, the demand for CBDFLS also increased simultaneously. In Table—3.3 the production of CBDFLS (Cross breed disease free layings) is shown. There has been fluctuations in the production of CBDFLS due to climatic disturbances in all the four districts. The overall growth rate is negative showing a decline in the productions of dfls. In all the four sample districts the trend is negative. It is also shown in Grap— 3.3.

Employment Generation

Sericulture provides high employment opportunities through its on form and off form activities. The involvement of labour is very high and the demand for both skilled and unskilled labour is increasing every year. The Table—3.4 presents the picture of the number of persons engaged in sericulture in the four Rayalaseema districts.

Table—3.4 Trends in Employment Generation in Sericulture in The sample Districts

Year	*District*				
	Anantapur	*Chittoor*	*Kurnool*	*Cuddapah*	*Andhra Pradesh*
1990-91	3,28,471	1,67,178	69,828	67,551	8,17,399
1991-92	3,42,837	1,78,431	72,820	71,137	8,86,600
1992-93	3,55,454	1,90,619	75,185	74,052	9,46,220
1993-94	3,65,090	1,99,177	78,771	78,771	9,98,514
1994-95	3,80,655	2,08,681	82,148	87,923	10,52,678
1995-96	3,97,485	2,26,050	87,923	84,150	11,14,839
1996-97	4,23,412	2,45,025	93,896	86,713	11,83,666
1997-98	4,42,552	2,59,127	96,294	89,958	12,38,820
1998-99	4,70,679	2,77,761	96,294	89,958	12,85,900
CGR	4.50	6.50	4.56	3.79	5.78

Source: Annual Administrative Reports, Directorate of Sericulture, Hyderabad. A.P.

Graph—3.3

Trends in production disease free layings—DFLS (in lakh no) in Rayalaseema region (1990-91 to 1998-99)

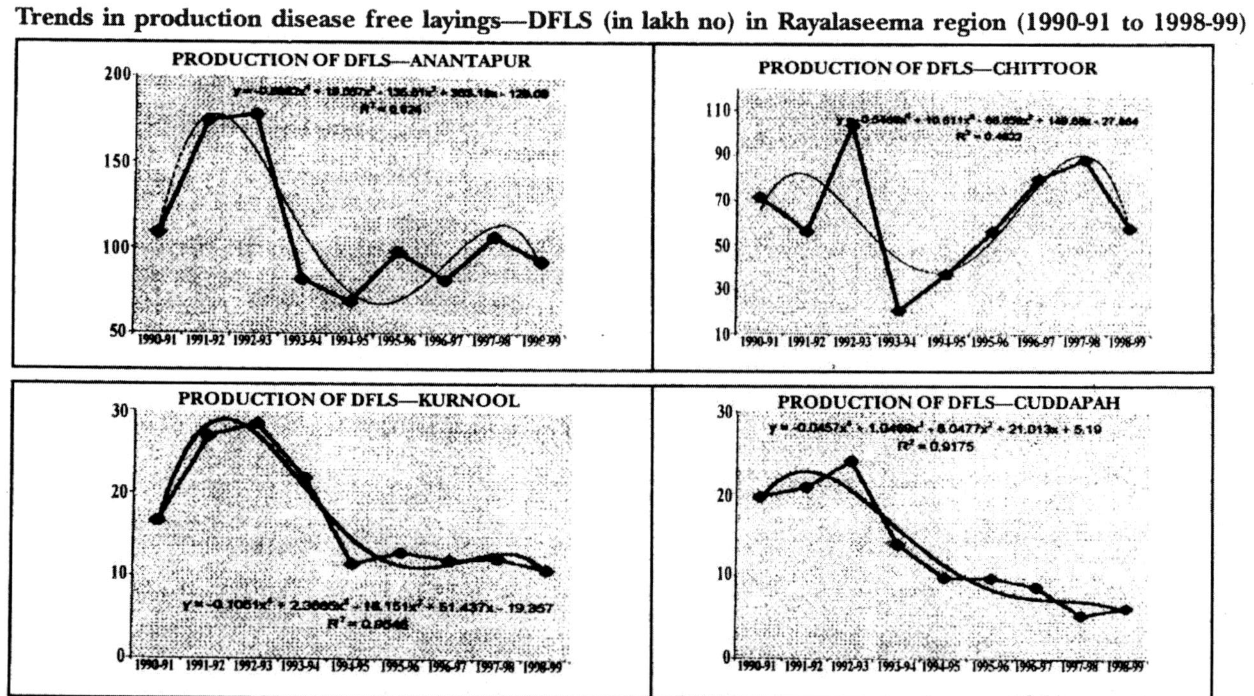

It is clear from the Table—3.4 that there has been a gradual raise in the number of persons employed in sericulture for the last nine years. It shows the enormous potential of the sericulture activity is providing job opportunities to the persons depending on agriculture sector for livelihood.

The overall compound growth rate in employment generation is at 5.78 per cent. Chittoor is showing highest growth rate (i.e. 6.50) followed by Cuddapah (3.79) and Kurnool (4.56). It is also depicted with the help of a Graph—3.4

Infrastructure Facilities Available

Provision of infrastructural facilities help for the development of any activity. The establishment of more number of facilities which are necessary for sericulture activity in Rayalaseema Region helped for the enormous growth of sericulture in this region. The detail are shown in Table—3.5.

Table—3.5

Sl. No.		*ATP*	*CTR*	*KNL*	*CDP*
1.	Technical Service centres (Extension)	23	22	6	4
2.	Technical Service centres (Extension)	3	–	–	–
3.	Govt. Silk Reeling unit	–	2	4	1
4.	Silkworm egg production centre	–	–	–	–
5.	P. Gov I seed forms	4+4	2+4		1+3
6.	P1 Gov I seed forms	1+1	1	6	1
7.	Govt. Seed Cocoon Markets	6	1+1	–	1+1
8.	Govt Cb cocoon Market	3	3	1	
9.	C3 station	1	1	–	–
10.	H. Demonstration forms	2	–	–	–
11.	Regional Training Centre	1	–	–	–
12.	Mobile former Training Unit	1-	–	–	–
13.	Gov I CB Grainages	6	6	2	2
14.	Chawkie rearing centres cum Mulberry cuttings supply centres	3-	–	7	–
15.	Farmer Training Centre	–	–	1	–
16.	H.Y.V. Nurseries	–	–	7	–

Source: Annual Administrative Reports, Directorate of Sericulture, Hyderabad, A.P.

Note: LR = Local Race, FR = Foreign Race.

Graph—3.4

Trends in employment generation through sericulture in Rayalaseema region (1990-91 to 1998-99)

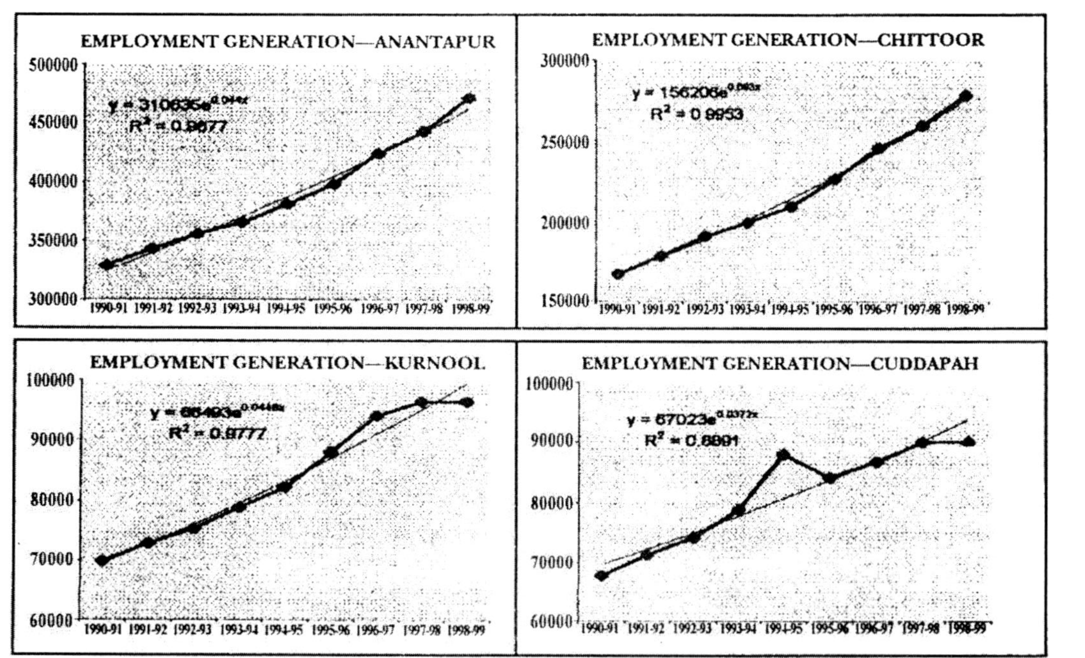

Women Development Programmes in Rayalaseema Region

In view of raising the participation of women in sericulture activities the Government of Andhra Pradesh has formulated number of programmes. The details of the programmes in Rayalaseema Region are furnished in the following pages.

In Anantapur district during 1994-95, nine women groups were formed. Seven groups were working in silkworm rearing and two groups in silk weaving. For these nine groups Rs. 3,75,000/- was released as working capital. During 95-96, three women groups were formed and Rs. 1,00,000 was released to rearing silk worms. During 96-97, 23 women groups were formed and Rs. 5,75,000 was released. During the above period women farmer meets we organised to train women in sericulture activity. Apart from this study tours are also organised to women groups. Dwcra women here given training at village level training programmes.

In Kurnool District, since 1995-96, a number of programmes for women like women'farmers meet, study tours, training in mulberry cultivation, silkworm rearing training to women sericulturists in new technologies here organised.

In Chittoor district, keeping the importance of women's involvement in sericulture activities the department has organised three days training programme to women sericulturists for adoption of technology in mulberry cultivation and silkworm rearing. Ninety sericulturists were trained for three days in the aspect of new technologies. The department has provided one time assistance of Rs. 25,000/- to Venkateswara Dwacra group women in B.N. Kandriga mandal of and another Rs. 25,000/- to 'Mahila Sericulture DWCRA group in Gangudrapalli village of Chandragiri mandal for purchasing chandrikas.

In Cuddapah district 150 women, interacted in sericulture here selected and among them 50 women were given training in sericulture. Apart from this study tours, training in new technologies were conducted.

SECTION—II

Socio-economic Profile of Sample Farmers

Socio-economic features will play a dominant role in decision making. The present section is documented with the socio-economic features of sample farmers. However only a limited number of these features have been taken into consideration in this study. Most important among them are the size of the land holdings, irrigation facilities, caste, type of family age composition and literacy. The present sample represents different sizes of land holdings and cultivators belonging to different levels of literacy. In view of the small mulberry landholdings of majority of sample farmers an acre is taken as a unit instead of a hectare for the purpose of analysis.

Categorisation of Farmers

The sample farmers are divided into three categories depending on the size of their landholdings. The Table—3.6 gives the details of sample farmers according to their landholdings.

Table—3.6 clearly gives a picture of categorisation of farmers in the sample districts. Out of the 240 sample farmers 32 farmers are marginal, 73 are small and 135 farmers are big. In this analysis, the farmers are categorised in such a way that, the farmers whose landholdings are 'below or equal to one hectare or 2.5 acres' as marginal farmers, whose land holdings are 'below or equal to two hectares or 5 acres, as small and whose landholdings are above 5 acres as big farmers. The sample has been collected totally on random basis. There are no marginal farmers in Anantapur and Kurnool districts in the sample area. And the average size of landings is 18.12 acres in Anantapur district and 7.32acres in Kurnool district followed by Cuddapah 6.22 acres and Chittoor 3.52 acres. The average size of landholdings among marginal farmers is 1.7 acres.

In the small farmers category there are 73 farmers, three in Anantapur, 25 in Chittoor, 18 in Kurnool and 27 in Cuddapah. Their average size of land-holdings is 4.22. In Anantapur it is 3.67 acres in Chittoor 3.58 acres, in Kurnool 4.78 acres and in Cuddapah 4.48 acres.

Among 135 big farmers in the sample, 57 are in Anantapur with an average size of landholdings of 18.88 acres, six are in Chittoor with 11.83 acres of average size of landholdings, 42 are in

Table—3.6 Distribution of sample farmers according to their category

Category of and the farmer	*Anantapur*			*Chittoor*			*Kurnool*			*Cuddapah*			*Total No*	*Average owned*
	1	*2*	*3*	*1*	*2*	*3*	*1*	*2*	*3*	*1*	*2*	*3*		
Marginal	–	–	–	29	51	1.74	–	–	–	3	6	2.00	32 (57acres)	1.78
Small	3	11	3.67	25	90	3.58	18	86	4.78	27	121	4.48	73 (308.0)	4.22
Big	57	1076	18.88	6	71	11.83	4.2	353	8.40	30	246	8.20	135 (1746)	12.93
Total	**60**	**1087**	**18.1[illegible]**	**60**	**211**	**3.52**	**60**	**439**	**7.32**	**60**	**373**	**6.22**	**240 2111 (acres)**	**8.8**

Note: 1. No. of Sample farmers.

2. Total Landholdings in acres.

3. Average landholdings in acres.

Source: Field data.

Kurnool district with 8.40 acres of average size of landholding and 30 were in Cuddapah with 8.20 acres of average size of landholdings. On an average out of 2111 acres of total land owned by all the sample farmers 8.8 acres is the average size of landholding. This shows the prosperity of farmers who are practising sericulture though as a subsidiary occupation.

Caste-wise Distribution of Sample Farmers

Table—3.7 gives the caste-wise distribution of sample farmers in the study area.

Table—3.7 Caste-wise distribution of sample farmers

Caste of the farmers	*District*				*Total*
	Anantapur	*Chittoor*	*Kurnool*	*Cuddapah*	
SC	13	13	19	19	64 (26.7)
ST	3	0	1	1	5 (2.1)
BC	14	18	13	18	63 (26.2)
OC	30	29	27	22	108 (45.00)
Total	**60**	**60**	**60**	**6**	**240 (100.00)**

Source: Field data.

It is clear from the Table—3.7 that out of 240 sample farmers 64 belong to scheduled castes (SCs), five belong to Scheduled Tribes (STs), 63 belong to Backward Castes (BCs) and 10 farmers belong to other castes (OCs). It is interesting to observe that in all the four districts the percentage of farmers belong to other castes is high (45 per cent). Though sericulture activity is mainly propagated for the people who belong to the weaker sections of the society, their involvement in this activity is less when compared to other castes. This may be due to their illiteracy, ignorance and non-availability of finances to invest in sericulture activity during initial stages.

Category and Caste-wise Distribution of Sample Farmers

The distribution of sample farmers according to their category is shown in the Table—3.8.

Table—3.8 Distribution of Sample farmers (Category and Caste-wise)

Category	*Anantapur*				*Chittoor*				*Kurnool*				*Cuddapah*				*Total*				*Total*
	SC	*ST*	*BC*	*OC*	*SC*	*ST*	*BC*	*OC*	*SC*	*ST*	*BC*	*OC*	*SC*	*ST*	*OB*	*OC*	*SC*	*ST*	*BC*	*OC*	
Marginal	-	-	-	-	4	0	11	14	-	-	-	-	2	-	1	-	6	-	12	14	32
Small	1	1	-	1	9	-	5	11	9	1	3	5	10	-	7	10	29	2	15	27	73
Big	12	2	14	29	-	-	2	4	10	-	10	22	7	1	10	12	29	3	36	67	135
Total	**13**	**3**	**14**	**30**	**13**	**-**	**18**	**29**	**19**	**1**	**13**	**27**	**19**	**1**	**18**	**22**	**64**	**5**	**63**	**108**	**240**

Source: Field data.

It is clear from the Table—3.8 that in Chittoor and Cuddapah district among marginal farmers category six belong to scheduled caste, 12 farmers belong to backward castes, 14 farmers belong to other castes. In small farmers category, 29 farmers belong the SCs, two farmers are STs, 15 farmers are BCs and 27 farmers belong to other castes. In Big farmers category 29 farmers belong to SCs, three belong to STs, 36 belong to backward castes and 67 farmers to other castes.

Age-wise Distribution of Sample Farmers

Table—3.9 gives a clear picture of age-wise distribution of sample farmers.

Table—3.9 Distribution of sample farmers according to their age groups

Age groups (in years)	*Anantapur*	*Chittoor*	*Kurnool*	*Cuddapah*	*Total*
15-25	-	2 (3.4)	-	2 (3.4)	4 (1.7)
26-35	8 (13.4)	12 (2.0)	2 (3.4)	24 (40)	46 (19.1)
36-45	37 (61.6)	31 (51.4)	40 (66.6)	23 (38.3)	131 (54.6)
>46	15 (25.0)	15 (25.0)	18 (30)	11 (18.3)	59 (24.6)
Total	**60 (100.0)**	**60 (100.00)**	**60 (100.0)**	**60 (100.0)**	**240 (100.0)**

Source: Field data.

It is clear from the Table—3.9 that there are four sericulturists in the age group of 15-25 out of 240 sample. In 26-35 age group there are 46 respondents and in 36-45 there are 131 sample sericulturists i.e. (54.6 per cent). In the age group of >46 years there are 59 sample farmers (24.6 per cent) out of 240 sample.

It can be observed from the above table that most of the sericulturists are (ie 54.6 per cent) in the age group of 36-45 followed by the 24.6 per cent in the age group of 46 and above. As sericulture has proved an one of the economically viable occupations, farmers who are already experienced with other crops are highly interested in practising this activity. The response among very young sericulturists i.e. 15-25 is only 1.7 per cent. Here it highlights the need of motivating younger generations towards this activity.

Religion

Table—3.10 shows about the religion-wise distribution of sample farmers in the study area.

Table—3.10 Distribution of sample farmers According to their Religion

Religion	*District*				*Total*
	Anantapur	*Chittoor*	*Kurnool*	*Cuddapah*	
Hindu	48 (80)	55 (91.6)	42 (70)	44 (73.4)	189 (78.8)
Muslim	-	1 (1.7)	11 (18.4)	8 (13.3)	20 (8.3)
Christian	12 (20)	4 (6.7)	7 (11.7)	8 (13.3)	31 (12.9)
Total	**60 (100)**	**60 (100)**	**60 (100)**	**60 (100)**	**240 (100.0)**

Source: Field data.

Note: Figures in parentheses indicate percentages to total number of farmers in each district.

It is clear from the Table—3.10 that there are 78.8 per cent farmers who belong to Hindu Religion. Christians form 12.9 per cent and Muslims form 8.3 per cent out of 240 sample farmers. In Anantapur district out of 60 sample farmers there are no Muslim sericulturists. Among Muslim sericulturists one is in Chittoor, 11 are in Kurnool 8 are in Cuddapah. Majority (189) of sericulturists belong to Hindu religion i.e. 80 per cent in Anantapur, 91.6 per cent in Chittoor, 70 per cent in Kurnool and 73.4 per cent in Cuddapah district.

Nature of Family

Table—3.11 gives a clear picture of nature of family of sample farmers.

Table—3.11 Distribution of the sample farmers according to their nature of family

Nature of the family	*District*				*Total*
	Anantapur	*Chittoor*	*Kurnool*	*Cuddapah*	
Joint	10 (16.6)	12 (20.0)	14 (23.3)	9 (15)	45 (18.8)
Nuclear	50 (83.4)	48 (80.0)	46 (76.7)	51 (85)	195 (81.2)
Total	**60 (100.00)**	**60 (100.00)**	**60 (100.00)**	**60 (100.00)**	**240 (100.0)**

Source: Field data.

Table—3.11 shows the nature of the family of sample farmers. Out of 240 sample farmers 195 farmers are living in nuclear families which accounts to 81.2 per cent, and 45 farmers are living in joint families (i.e 18.8 per cent. This is the impact of social transformation that is taking place in the society.

Education Levels of Sample Farmers

Education is another factor which influences the status of farmers. The following Table—3.12 gives a picture of the educational status of the sample farmers in the study area.

Table—3.12 Distribution of sample farmers according to their education levels

Status of Education	*Anantapur*	*Chittoor*	*Kurnool*	*Cuddapah*	*Total*
Illiterate	33 (55.0)	28 (46.6)	30 (50.0)	43 (71.6)	134 (55.8)
Primary	2 (3.3)	-	-	1 (1.7)	3 (1.3)
High School	24 (40.0)	31 (51.7)	28 (46.7)	16 (26.7)	99 (41.3)
Collegiate	1 (1.7)	1 (1.7)	2 (3.3)	-	4 (1.6)
Total	60 (100.0)	60 (100.0)	60 (100.0)	60 (100.0)	240

Source: Field data.

Note: Figures in parentheses indicate percentage to total number of farmers in each district.

It is clear from Table—3.12 that majority of farmers i.e 134 (55.8 per cent) in the study area illiterates. Only three of the sample farmers have primary education and, 99 farmers (41.3 per cent) have high school education. Only four farmers have collegiate education. In all the districts the number of illiterate farmers and those who possessed high school education is high.

Education and Caste-wise Distribution of Sample Farmers

Table—3.13 gives about the education and caste-wise distribution of sample farmers.

Table—3.13 Education and caste-wise Distribution of sample farmers

	ANANTAPUR					*CHITTOOR*					*KURNOOL*					*CUDDAPAH*					*Grand Total*				
	SC	*ST*	*BC*	*OC*	*Total*	*SC*	*ST*	*BC*	*OC*	*Total*	*SC*	*ST*	*BC*	*OC*	*Total*	*SC*	*ST*	*BC*	*OC*	*Total*	*SC*	*ST*	*BC*	*OC*	*Total*
Illiterate	9	2	9	13	33	7	-	11	10	28	11	1	6	12	30	12	1	15	15	43	39	4	41	50	134
Primary	-	-	-	2	2	-	-	-	-	-	-	-	-	-	-	1	-	-	-	1	1	-	-	2	3
High School	4	1	5	14	24	6	-	7	18	31	7	-	6	15	28	6	-	3	7	16	23	1	21	54	99
Collegiate	-	-	-	1	1	-	-	-	1	1	1	-	1	-	2	-	-	-	-	-	1	-	1	2	4
Total	**13**	**3**	**14**	**30**	**60**	**13**	**-**	**18**	**29**	**60**	**19**	**1**	**13**	**27**	**60**	**19**	**1**	**18**	**22**	**60**	**64**	**5**	**63**	**108**	**240**

Source: Field data.

Table—3.13 reveals that out of 240 sample farmers 39 SC farmers belong to illiterate group. 23 SC farmers have high school education. Among STs four farmers are illiterates and only one ST farmer is having high school education. None is having collegiate education among STs. Among BCs 41 farmers are illiterates 21 are having high school education. Among OCs 50 farmers are illiterates, two are having primary education, 54 are having high school education and only two have collegiate education.

Main Occupation of Sample Farmers

Table—3.14 shows about the distribution of sample farmers according to their main occupation.

Table—3.14 Distribution of sample farmers according to their main occupation

Occupation	*Anantapur*	*Chittoor*	*Kurnool*	*Cuddapah*	*Total*
Agriculture	60 (100.0)	46 (76.6)	60 (100.0)	55 (91.7)	221 (92.1)
Govt. Job	-	-	-	-	-
Business	-	2 (3.4)	-	-	2 (0.9)
Sericulture	-	12 (20)	-	5 (8.3)	17 (7.0)
	60 (100)	60 (100)	60 (100)	60 (100.0)	240 (100.0)

Source: Field data.

Note: Figures in parentheses indicate percentages to total number of farmers in each district.

Table—3.14 shows a clear picture about the distribution of farmers according to their main occupation. Out of four occupations listed, 221 are engaged with agriculture as their main occupation, which accounts to (92.1 per cent out of 240 sample). Two sample farmers are engaged in business as their main occupation. 17 farmers have sericulture as their main occupation. Only 17 sample farmers out of 240 are having sericulture as main occupation. It is because of fluctuation that are taking place very frequently in the cocoon yield and their prices and to some extent the involvement of skilled labourers in certain activities.

Main Occupation and Caste-wise Distribution of Sample Farmers

Table—3.15 gives a picture of distribution of sample farmers according to their main occupation and caste.

Table—3.15 shows that agriculture is the primary occupation for 221 farmers (i.e. for 92.1 per cent) in the study area. Only two farmers are having business also as primary occupation and for 17 farmers sericulture is main occupation. Among 64 SC farmers 62 farmers are engaged with agriculture as their primary occupation, one farmer took up business and another one farmer sericulture as their main occupation. Among STs all the five farmers are engaged in agriculture as their main occupation. Out of 63 BC farmers 55 farmers took up agriculture, one farmer is in business seven farmers took up sericulture as their main occupations. Among 108 OCs 99 farmers are engaged with agriculture and 9 farmers sericulture as have main occupation.

Distribution of Sample Farmers According to Their Main Occupation and Education

Table—3.16 gives detailed information about the sample farmers according to their main occupation and education.

Table—3.16 clearly shows the relation between education and selection of main occupation. It is interesting to note that majority of farmers i.e. 221 out of 240 irrespective of their educational status engaged in agriculture. Out of 221 farmers 126 are illiterates, 3 farmers are having primary education, and 88 farmers are having high school education and only four farmers are having collegiate education. This reveals that sericulture still needs some more campaigning and training to educated youth for motivating them to come forward to take up this activity as their main occupation.

Table—3.15 Occupation and caste-wise distribution of sample farmers

Main Occupation	*ANANTAPUR*					*CHITTOOR*					*KURNOOL*					*CUDDAPAH*					*Grand Total*				
	SC	*ST*	*BC*	*OC*	*Total*	*SC*	*ST*	*BC*	*OC*	*Total*	*SC*	*ST*	*BC*	*OC*	*Total*	*SC*	*ST*	*BC*	*OC*	*Total*	*SC*	*ST*	*BC*	*OC*	*Total*
Agriculture	13	3	14	30	60	12	-	12	22	48	19	1	13	27	60	18	1	16	20	55	62	5	55	99	221
Govt. Job	-	-	-	-	-	-	-	-	-	-	-	-	-	-	-	-	-	-	-	-	-	-	-	-	-
Business	-	-	-	-	-	1	-	1	-	2	-	-	-	-	-	-	-	-	-	-	1	-	1	-	2
Sericulture	-	-	-	-	-	-	-	5	7	12	-	-	-	-	-	1	-	2	2	5	1	-	7	9	17
Total	**13**	**3**	**14**	**30**	**60**	**13**	-	**18**	**29**	**60**	**19**	**1**	**13**	**27**	**60**	**19**	**1**	**18**	**22**	**60**	**64**	**5**	**63**	**108**	**240**

Source: Field data.

Table—3.16 Distribution of farmers according to their Main Occupation and Education

Main Occupation	*ANANTAPUR*					*CHITTOOR*					*KURNOOL*					*CUDDAPAH*					*Grand Total*				
	1	2	3	4	*Total*	1	2	3	4	*Total*	1	2	3	4	*Total*	1	2	3	4	*Total*	1	2	3	4	*Total*
Agriculture	33	2	24	1	60	23	-	22	1	46	30	-	28	2	60	40	1	14	-	55	126	3	88	4	221
Business	-	-	-	-	-	-	-	2	-	2	-	-	-	-	-	-	-	-	-	-	-	-	2	-	2
Sericulture	-	-	-	-	-	5	-	7	-	12	-	-	-	2	-	3	-	2	-	5	8	-	9	-	17
Total	**33**	**2**	**24**	-	**60**	**28**	-	**31**	-	**60**	**30**	-	**28**	**2**	**60**	**43**	**1**	**16**	-	**60**	**134**	**3**	**99**	**4**	**240**

Note: 1-Illiterate, 2-Primary, 3-High School, 4-College Education.

Irrigation Facilities

Table—3.17 shows about the irrigation facilities of sample farmers.

Table—3.17 Distribution of Sample farmers according to the availability of irrigation facilities

Nature of Irrigation facilities	*Anantapur*	*Chittoor*	*Kurnool*	*Cuddapah*	*Total*
Dug well	–	2 (3.3)	–	–	2 (0.8)
Dug and Bore well	–	2 (3.3)	–	–	2 (0.8)
Bore well	60	56 (93.4)	30 (50.0)	60	206 (85.8)
Bore well and Canal	–	–	30 (50.0)	–	30 (12.6)
Total	**60 (100)**	**60 (100)**	**60 (100)**	**60 (100)**	**240 (100.0)**

Source: Field data.

Note: Figures in parentheses indicate percentages to total number of farmers in each district.

The distribution of farmers according to the availability of irrigation facilities is presented in Table—3.17. The various sources of irrigation facilities available are dug well, dug cum bore well, bore well, bore well and canal in the sample area. Out of 240 sample farmers only 1.6 per cent are having dug well and dug cum bore well facility while others i.e. 85.8 per cent are having bore wells and 12.6 per cent are having bore wells and canal. Rayalaseema Region being drought area assured irrigation facilities can be available only through bore wells. As a result most of the farmers prefer drilling a bore well in their field for assured irrigation.

Caste and Irrigation Facilities

Table—3.18 shows about the availability of irrigation facilities to sample farmers according to their caste.

Table—3.18 Caste-wise distribution of farmers according to the irrigation facilities

Source of Irrigation	*ANANTAPUR*					*CHITTOOR*					*KURNOOL*					*CUDDAPAH*					*Grand Total*				
	SC	*ST*	*BC*	*OC*	*Total*	*SC*	*ST*	*BC*	*OC*	*Total*	*SC*	*ST*	*BC*	*OC*	*Total*	*SC*	*ST*	*BC*	*OC*	*Total*	*SC*	*ST*	*BC*	*OC*	*Total*
Dug Well	-	-	-	-	-	-	-	2	-	2	-	-	-	-	-	-	-	-	-	-	-	-	2	-	2
Dug well Bore well	-	-	-	-	-	-	-	-	2	2	-	-	-	-	-	-	-	-	-	-	-	-	-	2	2
Bore well	13	3	14	30	60	13	-	16	27	56	10	-	5	15	30	19	1	18	22	60	55	4	53	94	206
Bore well cum canal	-	-	-	-	-	-	-	-	-	-	9	1	8	12	30	-	-	-	-	-	9	1	8	12	30
Total	**13**	**3**	**14**	**30**	**60**	**13**	**-**	**18**	**29**	**60**	**19**	**1**	**13**	**27**	**60**	**19**	**1**	**18**	**22**	**60**	**64**	**5**	**63**	**108**	**240**

Source: Field data.

From the Table—3.18 it can be observed that out of 240 sample farmers, 206 are having bore well facility. Among them 55 farmers belong to SC category, four to ST category, 53 to BC category and 94 farmers to other castes. Only two BC farmers in Chittoor district i.e. (0.8 per cent) are depending on dug wells alone. Dug cum bore well facility is available for two farmers who belong to OC category in Chittoor. Almost all other sample farmers are having bore well, bore well and canal facility for irrigation.

Family Size

Table—3.19 reveals the family size of the sample farmers.

Table—3.19 Distribution of households according to the No. of members in the family

No. of members	Anantapur		Chittoor		Kurnool		Cuddapah		Total		Grand Total
	M	F	M	F	M	F	M	F	M	F	F
≤2	7	39	8	28	6	25	1	16	22	108	130
3 To 6	53	21	54	32	54	36	57	43	43	132	350
7 and above	8	0	0	0	2	-	2	1	1	13	14
Total	68	60	62	62	62	61	60	60	60	241	493

Source: Field data.

Note: M=Male, F= Female.

Table—3.19 shows that in all the four districts majority of the households contain 3 to 6 male members. Except in Anantapur district, the number of households with 3 to 6 female members is more than the families with ≤ 2 female members. The general observation is that the most dominating size of the family is 3 to 6.

Permanent Labour

Table—3.20 gives the details of permanent labour attached to the sample farmers' families.

Table—3.20 Distribution of family labour according to their number and sex

Size of Permanent Labour	*Anantapur*		*Chittoor*		*Kurnool*		*Cuddapah*		*Total*	
	M	*F*	*M*	*F*	*M*	*F*	*M*	*F*	*M*	*F*
1	7	40	24	24	13	49	22	12	88	123
2	47	18	17	17	46	11	30	2	140	30
3	5	-	-	-	1	-	-	-	6	-
Total	**59**	**58**	**41**	**41**	**60**	**60**	**52**	**14**	**212**	**153**

Source: Field data.

It is clear from the Table—3.20, that in Anantapur district among sample sericulturists there are seven families having one male permanent labourer. 47 families are having two male permanent labourers and fives families having three male permanent labourers. Similarly with regard to female labourers there are 40 families with one female labourer and 18 families with two female labourers.

In Chittoor district there are 24 families having one male and female permanent labourers and 17 families having two male and female permanent labourers.

Main Workers the Sample Farmers Families

Table—3.21 shows the details of availability of main workers in the sample farmers families.

Table—3.21 Distribution of Number of Main workers in the sample farmer's families

Main workers	*Anantapur*		*Chittoor*		*Kurnool*		*Cuddapah*		*Total*		*Grand Total*
	M	*F*	*M*	*F*	*M*	*F*	*M*	*F*	*M*	*F*	*F*
1	2	26	7	24	1	17	3	23	13	90	103
2	32	32	33	33	44	40	19	31	128	136	264
3	22	2	20	2	14	3	23	5	79	12	91
4	4	0	0	1	1	0	12	1	17	2	193
5	0	0	0	0	0	0	3	0	3	0	3
Total	60	60	60	60	60	60	60	60	240	240	480

Source: Field data.

Table—3.21 gives a clear picture of number of main workers in the sample farmers' family. There are 13 families in which there is only one male main worker available and 90 families in which only one female worker is available. The number of main workers both males and females is high in the category of two and three main workers. In the category of four main workers there are only 17 families having male workers and two families having four female workers and only 3 families with five male main workers.

Agricultural Main Workers According to Their Caste

Table—3.22 reveals that there are 29 male and 20 female main workers in the SC category in Anantapur district. Their total number is 152 male main workers and 97 female main workers in the SC category. In ST category there are 11 male main workers and five female main workers. Among BCs 161 are male workers and 106 are female main workers. Among OCs also their number is fairly good i.e. there are 265 male workers and 166 female main workers. Altogether there are 589 male main workers and 374 female main workers available in the study area.

Table—3.22 Number of Agricultural main workers according to their caste

Caste	*Anantapur*		*Chittoor*		*Kurnool*		*Cuddapah*		*Total*		*Grand Total*
	M	*F*	*M*	*F*	*M*	*F*	*M*	*F*	*M*	*F*	*F*
SC	29	20	28	20	43	32	52	25	152	97	249
ST	6	4	0	0	2	1	3	0	11	5	16
BC	34	20	40	31	29	25	58	30	161	106	267
OC	79	46	65	46	61	46	60	28	2 65	166	431
Total	**148**	**90**	**133**	**97**	**135**	**104**	**173**	**83**	**589**	**374**	**963**

Source: Field data.

Nature of Crops Grown by Sample Farmers

Table—2.3 shows a picture of other crops grown in the study area.

Table—3.23 Nature of crops grown in Rayalaseema districts

Crop	*Anantapur*	*Chittoor*	*Kurnool*	*Cuddapah*	*Total*
Paddy Area	51.5	55	72	71	249.5
Production (in quintals)	280.9	97.2	121	141.2	640.3
Value	18820	15960	17500	2 4,040	76320
Ground nut Area	273.5	12.8	104	35	424.8
Production	970.8	114	230	248.5	1563
Value	10032	9070	23691	34800	16788
Sugarcane Area	10	6	–	–	16
Production	100	51	–	–	151
Value	4100	2500	–	–	6600
Small Millets Area	24	12	59	34	129
Production	23	56	219	252	550
Value	26400	3400	14615	2835	4900

Source: Field data.

Note: (Area in acres, Production in quintals and value in Rs. in thousands).

It is clear from the Table—3.23 that the cropping pattern is not encouraging the farmers in this Region. Area under paddy and small millets which are food crops is very less the area under groundnut and sugarcane is also very less. The productivity levels are discouraging the farmers. Therefore the farmers are slowly shifting towards non-food and commercial crops as the net returns from these crops when compared to the traditional food crops are high.

Conclusion

Sericulture has been making rapid strides of progress in Andhra Pradesh state, particularly in Rayalaseema Region. Anantapur and Chittoor districts in the state have the unique distinction of producing mulberry silk. The climatic conditions prevailing in this Rayalaseema Region are more favourable for the development of mulberry cultivation and silkworm rearing. The infrastructural facilities available also made sericulture to achieve enormous growth rates in terms of area under mulberry cultivation, and cocoon production. Anantapur ranks first in the aspect of area under mulberry and cocoon production followed by Chittoor. Kurnool and Cuddapah districts come next in order.

REFERENCES

1. *Hand Book of Statistics, 1991-92*. Office of the Chief Planning Officer, District Statistical Office, Anantapur. p. 1.
2. Ibid. p. 1.
3. Chief Planning Officer, "*Hand Book of Statistics 1992-93,* Kurnool District, Kurnool, p. 1.
4. Ibid., p. 3.
5. Chief Planning Officer, "*Hand Book of Statistics 1992-93,* Cuddapah District, Cuddapah, p. 5.
6. Ibid. p. 38.
7. Chief Planning Officer, "*Hand Book of Statistics, 1993-94,* Chittoor District, Chittoor p. 1.
8. Ibid. p. 12.
9. Joint Director, Department Sericulture, Anantapur.
10. Ibid., p. 6.

4

Economics of Sericulture

Sericulture is a highly profitable activity and its profitability depends on the production of quality mulberry leaf and its conversion into quality cocoons at economic costs. An effort is made here to understand the economics and prospects of sericulture as an enterprise undertaken by the sample farmers in the study area. A number of variables which focus on the structure of costs and returns are presented here.

Adoption of Sericulture

The sericulture enterprise is undertaken by the sample households mainly because mulberry is a drought resistant plant and it brings more income in shorter intervals. This is an advantage it has over other crops. Sericulture has been practised by the sample sericulturists since more than six years in all the sample districts.

Size of Mulberry Land Holdings

The size of mulberry land holdings in the study area varies from 0.25 to 3.00 acres in general. The majority of land holdings are below one acre. The mulberry holdings are grouped into three categories viz., upto one acre, one to two acres and more than two acres for analysing the variables that influence sericulture activity. Categorisation of the mulberry land owned by the sample farmers is shown in Table—4.1.

Table—4.1 Categorisation of sample farmers according to their mulberry land holdings

Name of the district/ category farmer	*Anantapur*		*Chittoor*		*Kurnool*		*Cuddapah*		*Total*
	No. of Sericulturists								
	1	2	1	2	1	2	1	2	
<= 1.00 acre	11	15	20	30	13	14	22	19	144
1.2 acres	18	14	10	–	17	15	8	11	93
Above 2 acres	1	1	–	–	–	1	–	–	3
Total	**30**	**30**	**30**	**30**	**30**	**30**	**30**	**30**	**240**

Source: Field data.

Note: 1 = village 1, 2 = village =2 in the sample district.

It is clear from the Table—4.1 that the number of sample sericulturists decrease with an increase in the area under mulberry. There are 144 sample farmers practising sericulture in the category of upto one acre and 93 framers in the category of one to two acres and only three farmers in the category of above two acres.

Establishment of Mulberry Garden: (Initial Stage)

Mulberry being a perennial crop, the establishment of mulberry garden is a crucial factor in sericulture enterprise and there can be no compromise on the initial establishment cost. Profitability from sericulture largely depends in the production of mulberry leaf and its conversion in to cocoon production with the maximum cost. The average size of mulberry land holdings in our sample area happens to be 1.1, 1.3, 0.09 and 0.98 acres in Anantapur, Chittoor, Kurnool and Cuddapah district respectively. Hence one hectare of mulberry landholding is considered to be a large unit for cocoon production. Therefore, one acre is adopted as the economic unit for cocoon production in the analysis of sericulture economics. Mulberry being a leaf crop maximisation of leaf yield depends on factors like the variety of mulberry, irrigation, application of organic manure and fertilizers, inter cultivation etc. It is interesting to note that all the sample farmers in the districts of Rayalaseema have confirmed themselves to only two varieties of mulberry namely local and Kanva$_2$ (M5). More than 50 per cent of the respondents use kanva-2, 25 per cent of them grow both varieties and the remaining 25 per cent cultivate only the local variety. The type of plantation adopted in the study area is the 'row system' which is popularly known as the 'kolar system'. The plantation is made with cuttings. All the farms are irrigated by ground water through dug wells, bore wells and canals. Organic manure is applied once in a year to give fertility to the mulberry farm. The quantity of farm yard manure (FYM) varies from farmer to farmer. On an average 17 Cart loads of FYM are applied per acre in the sample districts. Chemical fertiliser is applied for every crop. The data pertaining to the various operations involved in the establishment and management of one acre irrigated mulberry garden is collected and the averages obtained are presented in Table—4.2.

Table—4.2 Initial establishment and management of one acre irrigated Mulberry Garden during first year

(Cost involved in Rupees)

S. No.	*Operation*	*Anantapur*		*Chittoor*		*Kurnool*		*Cuddpah*	
		L. days	*Cost*	*L. days*	*Cost*	*L. days*	*Cost*	*L. days*	*Cost*
1	*2*	*3*	*4*	*5*	*6*	*7*	*8*	*9*	*10*
A	**Establishment**								
1.	Land preparation	45	1800	45	1800	40	1600	45	1800
2.	Farm yard Manure (FYM)	17	1360	17	1360	17	1360	17	1360
3.	Bullock pair days involved	12	960	12	960	12	960	12	960
4.	FYM application	6	240	6	240	6	240	6	240
5.	Plantation								
a.	Plant cuttings	4CL	free	4CL	free	4CL	free	4CL	free
b.	Cutting preparation	4	160	4	160	4	160	4	160

(Table Contd...)

1	2	3	4	5	6	7	8	9	10
c.	Plantation	20	800	18	720	20	800	21	840
6.	Irrigation	20	800	20	800	20	800	20	800
7.	Weeding (2 times per crop)	30	1200	30	1200	28	1120	28	1120
8.	Miscellaneous	–	300	–	300	–	300	–	300
	Total	**125**	**7620**	**123**	**7540**	**118**	**7340**	**124**	**7580**
B.	**Management**								
1.	Inter cultivation (3 times)	60	2400	60	2400	55	2200	54	2160
2.	Irrigation	40	1600	40	1600	35	1400	35	1400
3.	Fertiliser cost								
a.	Complex	100 kg	500	100 kg	500	100 kg	500	100 kg	500
b.	Urea	50 kg	150	50 kg	150	50 kg	150	50 kg	150
4.	Fertiliser application	5	200	5	200	5	200	5	200
5.	Leaf harvest	50	2000	50	2000	45	2000	40	2000
6.	Non-recurring	–	400	–	400	–	300	–	350
	Total	**155**	**7250**	**155**	**7250**	**140**	**6750**	**135**	**6760**
	Grand Total	**280**		**278**		**258**		**259**	

Source: Field data.

CL = Cart Load.

L .days = Labour days.

Table—4.2 shows the various operations and the cost involved to establish and manage one acre of irrigated mulberry garden. The establishment of one acre of it works out to Rs. 7620/- in Anantapur district, Rs. 7540/- in Chittoor district, Rs. 7340/- in Kurnool district and Rs.7580/- in Cuddapah district. The major items involved in the exercise are land preparation, application of farm yard manure and weeding. The mulberry garden once established is expected to give yield for 12 to 15 years. Hence, the non-recurring expenditure on the initial establishment cost is Rs. 300/- in all the sample districts.

The management cost of established mulberry garden during the first year is Rs. 7250/- in Anantapur, and Chittoor, Rs. 6750/- in Kurnool district and Rs. 6760/- Cuddapah district. During the first year the number of crops harvested is.small and the productivity of the crop is also low. Over the years, however, the sericulturists have gained knowledge and experience and improved their performance and productivity levels.

Management of Established Mulberry Garden

As already mentioned the mulberry garden once established yields for a long period. The recurring expenditure involved in the maintenance of one acre of established, irrigated mulberry garden is shown in Table—4.3.

Table—4.3 Recurring expenditure on one acre of established irrigated mulberry garden from second year onwards

(Cost involved in Rupees)

S. No.	*Operation*	*Anantapur*		*Chittoor*		*Kurnool*		*Cuddapah*	
		M. Days	*Cost*	*M. Days*	*Cost*	*M. Days*	*Cost*	*M. Days*	*Cost*
1	*2*	*3*	*4*	*5*	*6*	*7*	*8*	*9*	*10*
1.	Cultivation expenses (Ploughing, making ridges and furrows and weeding)	85	3400	80	3200	75	3000	80	3200
2.	Irrigation	12 BPD	960	10	800	10	800	10	800
3.	Farm yard Manure (FYM)	17 CL	1360	17 CL	1360	16 CL	1280	16 CL	1280
4.	Application (FYM)	6	240	6	240	5	200	5	200
5.	Cost of Chemical fertilizer								
a.	300 kg. Complex	-	1500	-	1500	-	1500	-	1500
b.	150 kg Urea	-	450	-	450	-	450	-	450
6.	Application Chemical fertilizer	8	320	6	240	6	240	5	200

(Table Contd...)

1	2	3	4	5	6	7	8	9	10
7.	Leaf harvest	120	4800	115	4600	110	4400	110	4400
8.	Non-recurring expenditure	–	300	–	300	–	250	–	250
	Total		**13,330**	–	**12,690**	–	**12,120**	–	**12,280**

Source: Field data.

CL: Cart Load

BPD: Bullock Pair days.

M.days: Man days.

From Table—4.3, it is clear that the estimated recurring expenditure on the management of an established garden is around Rs. 13,330/- in Anantapur district and Rs. 12,690 in Chittoor district and Rs. 12,120/- and Rs. 12,280 in Kurnool and Cuddapah districts. With the involvement of family labour, the expenditure on mulberry cultivation can be reduced considerably. The expenditure in Anantapur district is high during second year onwards. The farmers in this district are very particular about the mulberry garden and they do not want to make any compromises in its establishment cost, so as to maintain the quality of leaf. Expenditure incurred on maintenance of one acre irrigated mulberry garden is shown in Table—4.4.

Table—4.4 shows that the actual expenditure incurred by the sericulturists of different size groups varies from Rs. 5,650/- to Rs. 5,600 in Anantapur, Rs. 5,925/- to Rs. 5,890/- in Chittoor, Rs. 5,755 to 5,695 in Kurnool district and Rs. 5,725 to Rs. 5,785 in Cuddapah district. Infact on an average, the formers incur an expenditure of Rs. 5,650/- (42 per cent) of the estimated cost (Rs. 13,330) in Anantapur district, Rs. 5,895/- (46.5 per cent) of the estimated cost, in Chittoor district, Rs. 5,727/- (47.3 per cent), of the estimated cost in Kurnool district and Rs. 5,763/- (47 per cent) of the estimated cost in Cuddapah district.

The mulberry plantation will be fully established in one year and reaches its maximum yield from the second year onwards under irrigated conditions. The leaf yield is more or less uniform in all the seasons in the irrigated mulberry. The mulberry leaf yield obtained by the sample sericulturists is presented in Table—4.5.

Table—4.4 Expenditure incurred on Maintenance of one acre irrigated Mulberry Garden

(in Rupees)

S. No.	Particulars	Mulberry holdings size in Acres											
		Anantapur			Chittoor			Kurnool			Cuddapah		
		upto 1.00	1.00 to 2.00	>2.00	upto 1.00	1.00 to 2.00	>2.00	upto 1.00	1.00 to 2.00	>2.00	upto 1.00	1.00 to 2.00	>2.00
1.	Cultivation												
a.	Human Labour	1600	1900	1900	1800	2000	2050	1850	2050	2100	1800	2050	2100
b.	Bullock Labour	500	200	200	525	210	220	530	210	215	525	220	210
2.	FYM	1000	800	600	1050	810	620	1075	820	630	1050	810	600
3.	Chemical fertilisers	1750	1900	2000	1750	1950	2050	1700	1950	2000	1700	1900	2050
4.	Non-recurring	400	400	400	400	400	400	300	300	300	350	350	350
5.	Miscellaneous	400	500	500	400	500	550	300	400	450	300	450	475
	Total	**5650**	**5700**	**5600**	**5925**	**5870**	**5890**	**5755**	**5730**	**5695**	**5725**	**5780**	**5785**
	Pooled	5650			5895			5727			5763		

Source: Field data.

Table—4.5 Mulberry leaf produced per acre and its production cost per kg

Size of Mulberry land holdings (in Ac)	*Anantapur*		*Chittoor*		*Kurnool*		*Cuddapah*	
	Quantity in kg.	*Cost of production per kg. (in Rs.)*	*Quantity kg.*	*Cost of production per kg. (in Rs.)*	*Quantity kg.*	*Cost of production per kg. (in Rs.)*	*Quantity kg.*	*Cost of production per kg. (in Rs.)*
Up to1.00	9,000	0.62	8,800	0.67	8,000	0.71	8,150	0.70
1.01 to 2.00	8,650	0.65	8,050	0.72	7,650	0.74	7,800	0.74
> 2.00	10,110	0.55	9,540	0.61	9,100	0.62	9,000	0.64
Pooled	9,253	61	8,797	67	8250	69	8137	70

Source: Field data.

It is evident from Table—4.5 that is Anantapur district on an overage the quantity of leaf produced per acre is 10,110 kg. which is considerably higher than 9,000 kg. produced in Cuddapah in the Category of farmers cultivating mulberry in more than two acres. The production cost of mulberry is least in all categories of farmers in Anantapur district, when compared to other district. It is interesting to note that those who produce more quantity of leaf have incurred less expenditure than those producing less.

Silkworm Rearing

Silkworm rearing is a cottage activity carried on by the sericulturists in his/her own house or in a separate room specially meant for it, as it requires a lot of attention. It involves a complicated process when various technical procedures are to be understood and implemented for high productivity. It demands a substantial amount of managerial skills on the part of the rearers and their own experience forms a good guide.

The rearing starts with the purchase of silkworm eggs called disease-free-layings (dfts) or industrial seed normally at the cost of Rs. 250/- per hundred dfts. Both Bivoltine and Multivoltine silkworm eggs are available to the rearers. Sericulturists buy these eggs from government grainages or licensed seed-producers. In the present sample all the sericulturists rear 'Multivoltine' variety of silkworms only because of its advantage to withstand against all odds of fluctuations in temperature, unhygienic conditions in rearing sheds etc.

Place of Rearing

The rearing of silkworms has to take place on protected premises to avoid diseases and disturbances. The details of the rearing place of silkworms are collected from the sample households and tabulated in Table—4.6.

Table—4.6 Nature of rearing place of silkworms

Size of Mulberry landholdings in acres	*Anantapur*				*Chittoor*				*Kurnool*				*Cuddapah*			
	1	2	3	4	1	2	3	4	1	2	3	4	1	2	3	4
Up to 1 acre	2	19	5	26 (43.4)	11	21	17	49 (81.7)	4	17	6	27 (45.00)	14	20	7	41 (68.3)
1 to 2 acres	8	15	9	32 (53.3)	2	5	3	10 (16.6)	5	17	10	32 (53.3)	5	13	1	19 (31.7)
> 2 acres	2	-	-	2 (3.3)	-	-	-	1 (2.7)	-	1	-	1 (1.7)	-	-	-	-
Total	**12**	**34**	**14**	**60 (100)**	**14**	**26**	**20**	**60 (100)**	**9**	**35**	**16**	**60 (100)**	**19**	**33**	**8**	**60 (100)**

Source: Field data.

Note: 1. Rearing shed in the farm.

2. Separate Rearing shed in the house.

3. Rearing shed in the dwelling house.

4. Total number of farmers.

(Figures in parentheses indicate percentages).

It is evident from Table—4.6 that in all the districts more than 60 per cent of the sericulturists rear silkworms in a separate rearing shed in the house. Only a few of them have separate rearing shed in the farms. Majority of the farmers in these sample districts rear silkworms in separate sheds built in the dwelling houses. As an unfortunate consequence of this practice there is frequent occurrence of diseases infecting the silkworms.

Therefore, a separate shed is very much essential to protect the silkworms from infections and to improve their quality and productivity. In the present study it is worked out that the investment on a rearing shed comes to around Rs.30,000/- with two per cent depreciation per year and the recurring expenditure comes to Rs.600/- per annum towards the cost of the rearing shed.

Rearing Equipment

Apart from a separate shed required for silkworms rearing it also requires a specific type of equipment which can be used for no other purpose. The details of the rearing equipment and the investment on them are presented in Table—4.7.

Table—4.7 Investment on Rearing Equipment

S. No.	*Equipment*	*Total Cost (in Rs.)*	*Utility years*	*Depreciation per year (in Rs.)*
1.	Wooden rearing Trays (15)	1,500	10	150
2.	Chawkie rearing stand	150	10	15
3.	Leaf chopping boards (2)	350	10	35
4.	Chopping knives (2)	100	4	25
5.	Rearing stands (8)	4,500	10	45
6.	Ant wells (36)	400	10	40
7.	Bamboo round trays (80)	2,000	3	666
8.	Leaf Chamber (1)	450	10	45
9.	Bed cleaning nets (16)	700	3	233
10.	Foam pads (20)	100	5	20
11.	Bamboo montages (75)	7,000	3	2,333
	Total	**17,250**		**3,607**

Source: Field data.

It is clear from the Table—4.7, that the items like wooden rearing trays, rearing stands, bamboo round trays and bomboo mountages are prominent items of fixed cost. The non-recurring expenditure on the fixed cost of rearing equipment works out to be Rs. 3,607/-. Among the sample farmers a few rearers hire a certain number of bamboo mountages (Chandrikas) on which cocoons are spun. These Chandrikas are required for two or three days during the last stages of rearing. Hiring is, therefore, a matter of assembling a sufficient number of sets from neighbours though the hiring business is not a specified activity in these districts.

Quantity of Disease-free-layings Reared

Sericulturists select a certain quantity of disease-free laying (dfls) for rearing depending on the size of their mulberry garden. The data collected from the sample households with regard to the annual quality of dfls reared per acre, the average number of rearings undertaken in a year and the quantity reared per acre are presented in Table—4.8.

From the Table—4.8 it is evident that the annual average quantity of dfls reared per unit area of one acre is worked out to be 1,200, in Anantapur and Chittoor Districts and 1,150 and 1,100 in Kurnool and Cuddapah Districts respectively. However the difference of 850 to 900 dfle over a year is not much significant. In all the districts the rearers who have one to two acres of land under mulberry cultivation rear less when compared to the other two groups of rearers. Rearers who own mulberry land holdings more than two acres rear more quantity of dfls.

On an average all the sericulturists harvest five crops per year. The average quantity of dfls reared per crop is 250 dfls in all mulberry size holdings of Anantapur district, 240 dfls in Chittoor district, 230 and 220 in Kurnool and Cuddapah districts respectively.

Expenditure Involved in Rearing

The analysis in earlier paragraphs shows, that the average quantity of disease free layings reared per crop is 250, 240, 230 and 220 in Anantapur, Chittoor, Kurnool and Cuddapah respectively. The estimated expenditure involved in each rearing is collected from the sample sericulturists and the averages are worked out for rearing of 200-250 dfls is presented in Table—4.9.

Table—4.8. Quantity of silkworms reared per household

Size of Mulberry Landholdings Group (in Ac)	*Anantapur*			*Chittoor*			*Kurnool*			*Cuddapah*		
	Annual quantity	*Average No. of rearings*	*Average Quantity reared per crop*	*Annual quantity*	*Average No. of rearings*	*Average Quantity reared per crop*	*Annual quantity*	*Average No. of rearings*	*Average Quantity reared per crop*	*Annual quantity*	*Average No. of rearings*	*Average Quantity reared per crop*
Up to 1.00	1250	5	270	1260	5	260	1250	5	262	1050	5	256
1.00 to 2.00	1100	5	220	1050	5	210	1000	5	200	980	5	196
> 2.00	1350	5	250	1300	5	252	1310	5	230	1280	5	210
Pooled	1200	5	250	1200	5	240	1150	5	230	1100	5	220

Source: Field data.

Table—4.9 Expenditure involved in Rearing of 200-250 dfls

(in Rs.)

S. No.	Description	*Anantapur*		*Chittoor*		*Kurnool*		*Cuddapah*	
1.	Cost of dfls								
	(a) Rs.250 per 100 dfls	-	625	-	625	-	625	-	625
2.	Cost of Labour wage								
	(a) First & Second Instar	24	960	19	760	22	880	16	640
	(b) Third Instar	22	880	15	600	16	640	24	960
	(c) Fourth Instar	32	1280	31	1240	27	1080	29	1160
	(d) Fifth Instar								
	(e) Collection of ripend worms and mounting	159	6360	159	6360	160	6400	59	6360
3.	Paraffin paper formalin, news paper transportation charges etc.	-	400	-	400	-	400	-	400
	Total	**237**	**10505**	**224**	**9985**	**225**	**10025**	**228**	**10145**

Source: Field data.

Note: Wages paid at Rs. 40/- per man day.

The Table—4.9, shows that, on an average the cost involved for rearing 200-250 dfls works out to be Rs. 10,505/-, Rs. 9,985/-, Rs. 10,025/- and Rs. 10,145/- in the Anantapur, Chittoor Kurnool and Cuddapah districts respectively. It is inclusive of the depreciation on the rearing place and non-recurring expenditure on the rearing equipment.

As already mentioned, the rearing activity is labour intensive and accordingly the estimated expenditure on the labour component is also higher than the other inputs involved in this activity. The involvement of family labour considerably reduces the expenditure on labour. The actual expenditure incurred by the sample rearers is indicated in Table—4.9. Expenditure incurred on rearing in a year is presented in Table—4.10.

Table—4.10 Expenditure incurred on rearing in a year (in Rupees) mulberry size class in acres

Particulars	*Anantapur*	*Chittoor*	*Kurnool*	*Cuddapah*
Cost of dfls reared	3,125	3,125	3,125	2,625
Expenditure on labour	47,400	44,500	45,000	45,600
Non-recurring expenditure	4,000	4,000	4,000	4,000
Miscellaneous	1,500	1,500	1,500	1,500
Total	**56,125**	**53,150**	**53,625**	**53,725**

It is clear from the Table—4.10 that the rearing expenditure involved on rearing of silkworms in a year is at Rs. 56,125/- in Anantapur district Rs. 53,150/- in Chittoor Rs. 53,625/- in Kurnool and Rs. 53,725/- in Cuddapah District. The expenditure spent on labour is very high in all these sample districts. But the point to be noticed there is, it is the expenditure spent together on both own and hired labour. As per the study the involvement of hired labour is around 52 per cent in all the activities. Therefore there will be considerable reduction on the amount spent in actual rupees on labour. The involvement of female labour is 45 to 61 per cent. But these creation of mandays shows how the sericulture activity keeps all the family members busy throughout the year without any slack season or giving idle time for farmers.

Cocoon Yield: While studying the different parameters of sericulture we have to keep in mind the relationship between the productivity levels and the levels of efficiency achieved in the cultivation of mulberry and silkworm rearing. The levels of physical performance attained by the rearers of different mulberry size groups are analysed in terms of the yield derived by them. The cocoon yield and the performance levels of the rearers of different size groups are furnished in Table—4.11.

Table—4.11 gives a clear picture of the average yield of cocoons per acre per annum in the sample districts. The reares of more than two acres of mulberry garden have drawn the maximum yield of 45 kgs per 100 dfls in Kurnool district, 43 kgs in Chittoor district and 30 and 38 kgs per 100 dfls in Anantapur and Cuddapah district. However the average cocoon yield however is the same ranging between 40 kgs to 43 kgs in all the sample districts. The difference between the total dfls reared and the dfls harvested in normally accounted for by the failure of crops. The average success rate of the crops increases the cocoon yield. However there is 20-25 per cent of failure rate in the study area.

The leaf cocoon ratio is a measure to identity the efficiency levels in rearing. To derive the yield of one Kilogram of cocoons, the leaf used should be around 30 kgs. Anything less than this indicates efficient use of the leaf and anything more than this level indicates less efficient or inefficient use of the leaf. In the districts under study the efficiency is seen to increase with the increase in the area under mulberry. On an average, the rearers of the Kurnool, Cuddapah and Chittoor district showed greater efficiency when compared to Anantapur district.

Costs and Returns on one Acre of Irrigated Mulberry Garden in a Year

The success of sericulture enterprise depends on the level of profits it enjoys. The returns obtained by sericulturists act as a measure in determining the economic viability of sericulture activity. Therefore an attempt is made to analyse the cost and net returns from the sericulture enterprise in the study area. Table—4.12 gives a clear picture of the costs and returns on one acre of irrigated mulberry garden.

Table—4.11 Cocoon yield and performance levels of sericulturists in rearing activity

Particulars	*Anantapur*				*Chittoor*				*Kurnool*				*Cuddapah*			
A	1	2	3	4	1	2	3	4	1	2	3	4	1	2	3	4
Total dfls reared per acre	1330	1311	1360	1337	1300	1350	1360	1337	1312	1343	1350	1335	1308	1300	1350	1319
Total Cocoon yield obtained per acre in kgs.	300	315	375	330	330	340	380	350	320	340	380	347	300	340	360	333
Yield per 100 dfls in kgs.	23	24	28	25	25	25	24	25	24	25	28	26	23	26	27	25
Leaf cocoon ratio	30	27	28	28	27	24	25	25	25	23	24	24	27	23	25	25
B																
Total dfls harvested per acre	700	800	950	817	742	800	900	814	910	872	850	877	746	812	935	831
Percentage of harvested dfls to total dfls	53	61	70	61	57	59	66	61	69	65	63	66	57	62	69	63
Yield per 100 dfls harvested in kgs	43	39	40	41	44	43	42	43	35	39	45	40	40	42	38	63

Source: Field data.

Note: 1, 2, 3 –Mulberry landholdings size groups.

4 –Pooled quantity.

It is evident from the Table—4.12 that the total expenditure varies from Rs. 15,908/ to Rs. 16,155/- in the sample districts. It is interesting to note that the total expenditure incurred on rearing of silkworms is more than the expenditure on mulberry cultivation in all the sample districts. It comes to 63 to 65 per cent of the total expenditure. This is due to the delicate nature of the silkworms, the rearing activity demands utmost care and skill. Hence, sericulturists have to depend on skilled labour. Therefore the expenditure on rearing increases considerably. However, the precautions taken result in good yield of cocoons.

Table—4.12 Costs and returns on one acre of irrigated mulberry garden

(in Rs.)

S.No.	*Particulars*	*Anantapur*	*Chittoor*	*Kurnool*	*Cuddapah*
A	Expenditure				
a.	Production of mulberry leaf	51,650(35)	5,895(37)	5,727(36)	5,763(36)
b.	Silkworm rearing	10,505 (65)	9,985 (63)	10,025 (64)	10,145 (64)
c.	Total	16,155 (100)	15,880 (100)	15, 752 (100)	15,908 (100)
B	Quantity of cocoons produced (in kgs)	330	350	380	333
C	Returns in Rs. Through sale of cocoons at Rs.140/- per kg	46,200	49,000	53,200	46,620
D.	Net Returns (in Rs.)	30,045	33,120	37,448	30,712

Source: Field data.

Note: Figures in parentheses indicate percentages to total.

With regard to the net income Kurnool district's performance is highly excellent. Here the sericulturists are able to obtain 37,448 per acre per year, whereas the lowest is Anantapur district at Rs. 30,045/-. The area under mulberry and the sericulture activity though it is widespread all over the district the net result is not giving any encouraging picture. The districts Kurnool and Cuddapah are picking up slowly and the sericulturists in these areas are putting more efforts to obtain good yield of cocoons and thereby good returns.

Marketing of the Cocoons: After rearing of silkworms and obtaining cocoons, the next major activity is taking them to markets for selling. The worm in the cocoon comes out of the cocoon after 3 or 4th day of its spinning is over. Then the cocoons become waste for spinning. Therefore marketing becomes an important aspect for every sericulturist. In the sample districts, sericulturists usually prefer to take them to nearby markets to reduce the percentage of damage and transport costs. Sericulturists in Anantapur take their cocoons to Kadiri, Hindupur, Dharmavaram, if time permits to Karnataka State markets like Kanakapura, Vijayapura, Ramanagara Siddlagatta and Chintamani. Sericulturists in Chittoor district carry their cocoons to Madanapalli, Chandragiri, Palamaneru, Nagari and Karnataka State markets. Sericulturists in Kurnool district sell their cocoon in Atmakur and Kurnool markets and in Cuddapah district, Sericulturists take their cocoons to Rayachoti and Madanapalli Markets.

Training to Sample Sericulturists: As sericulture activity is a new activity to the farmers, to develop their interest towards this occupation and to provide necessary skills to grow mulberry graden and to rear silkworms the government has designed training programmes. The details of the sericulturists who have undergone training in the sample districts is shown in Table—4.13.

Table—4.13 Details of sericulturists undergone training

District	*Category of sericulturists (in acres)*	*Yes*	*No*	*Total*
Anantapur	<=1-00	12	14	26
	1-2	14	18	32
	above 2.00	1	1	2
Chittoor	<=1-00	38	12	50
	1-2	4	6	10
	above 2.00	–	–	–
Kurnool	<=1.00	7	20	27
	1-2	13	19	32
	above 2.00	–	1	1
Cuddapah	<=1.00	12	29	41
	1-2	1	17	18
	above 2.00	1	–	1
Total		**103 (43)***	**137 (57)***	**240 (100)***

Source: Field data.

Note: *Figures in parentheses indicate percentages.

It is clear from the Table—4.13 that majority of the farmers in Kurnool and Cuddapah have not undergone any training. On an overage 43 per cent of the sample farmers have not taken training. Training helps to improve the performance levels of sericulturists. But though a good number of training programmes is offered sericulturists in the sample area are not aware of them. It reveals that there is still a need to motive farmers towards sericulture activity in these districts.

In the Table—4.14 the loans and subsidies received by sample sericulturists is shown.

It is clear from Table—4.14 that out of 240 sample farmers 53 per cent have taken loans from government to undertake sericulture. The subsidy facility offered to encourage sericulturists is also availed by 55 per cent of farmers. In this context the sericulturists express their opinion with regard to their wish to undertake more area under sericulture. Their responses are shown in Table—4.15.

It is evident from the Table—4.15 that 72 per cent of the sample sericulturists wish to undertake more area under mulberry cultivation. it is interesting to note that in Chittoor district all the sample farmers in the study area expressed their willingness to extend their mulberry landholdings.

With regard to the displacement of crops like paddy, ragi, jowar, sugarcane, sunflower and small millets, 64 per cent of the sample sericulturists agreed that some of the food crops are displaced due to sericulture activity. As mulberry plant is drought resistant and yields at least minimum guarantee to sustain even during severe drought conditions majority of the farmers are willing to take up mulberry cultivation on full-fledged basis.

Table—4.14 Details of loans and subsidies received by sample sericulturists

District	Category of Sericulturists	Loan Received			Subsidy Received		
		Yes	No	Total	Yes	No	Total
	(In acres)						
Anantapur	< = 1.00	11	15	26	14	12	26
	1-2	20	12	32	24	8	32
	above 2.00	2	–	2	2	–	2
Chittoor	< = 1.00	35	15	50	34	16	50
	1-2	5	5	10	5	5	10
	above 2.00	–	–	–	–		
Kurnool	< = 1.00	15	9	24	16	10	26
	1-2	19	13	32	19	13	32
	above 2.00	3	1	4	–	2	2
Cuddapah	< = 1.00	14	27	41	14	27	41
	1-2	4	14	18	4	14	18
	above 2.00	–	1	1	–	1	2
Total		**128 (53)***	**112 (47)***	**240 (100)***	**132 (55)***	**108 (45)***	**240 (100)***

Source: Field data.

Note: *Figures in parentheses indicate percentages.

Table—4.15 Sericulturists responses to undertake more area under mulberry cultivation

District	*Category (in acres)*	*Yes*	*No*	*Total*
Anantapur	<=1.00	24	2	26
	1-2	14	18	32
	above 2.00	1	1	2
Chittoor	< = 1.00	50	–	50
	1-2	10	–	10
	above 2.00	–	–	–
Kurnool	< = 1.00	23	4	27
	1-2	11	21	32
	above 2.00	–	1	1
Cuddapah	< = 1.00	30	11	41
	1-2	10	8	18
	above 2.00	–	1	1
Total		**173 (72)**	**67 (28)**	**240 (100)**

Source: Field data.

Note: Figures in parentheses indicate percentages.

Conclusion

Sericulture is a highly profitable activity and its profitability depends on the production of leaf and its conversion into quality cocoons at economic costs. The sericulture activity is undertaken by the sample households mainly because mulberry is a drought resistant plant and it brings more income in shorter intervals. The majority of the landholdings under mulberry in this region are below one acre. Mulberry being a perennial crop once it established it yields for 12 to 15 years. The establishment costs are more during initial stages. Silkworm rearing is a delicate activity and to be carried over with utmost care. the involvement of female labour both hired and own can he seen in the activities of both mulberry cultivation and silkworm rearing. The cocoons are taken to the nearby local markets and adjacent Karnatake state markets. Nearly 57 per cent of the farmers have not undergone any training and majority of the sample sericulturists gave their willingness to extend the land under mulberry cultivation.

5

Employment Generation for Women Through Sericulture

Sericulture has been recognised as an activity where the generation of employment opportunities is very high. Being agro-based in nature sericulture provides job opportunities for males and females in a variety of activities involved. Sericulture activity creates employment generation in two ways. 1. Mulberry cultivation and Silkworm rearing and 2. Silk weaving, dyeing, printing etc. This present study has been confined up to silkworm rearing. Therefore the employment generated through the various activities involved in 'mulberry cultivation' and 'silkworm rearing' are examined and presented in the following pages.

Moreover the participation of women is either equal or even more than the men folk in sericulture activities. They take part in mulberry cultivation and silkworm rearing activities in addition to their multifarious responsibilities at home. To examine the role of women in sericulture activities an attempt has been made in this chapter. As the study is confined only upto to the generation of employment opportunities in agriculture sector, the activities that come under mulberry cultivation have been categorised as: 1. Ploughing 2. Levelling 3. Weeding 4. Farmyard manure application and 5. Chemical manure application. All the other activities like land preparation, selection of mulberry variety, planting, pruning, irrigation inter-cultivation, leaf harvestings and storage of leaves come under these five major categories. In the presentation the averages of mandays created have been rounded to the nearest whole number.

Ploughing

The mandays generated in ploughing per acre of mulberry per crop is presented in the following Table—5.1.

Table—5.1 Average mandays generated in ploughing activity

(in Mandays)

District	*Village*	*1*	*2*	*3*	*4*
Anantapur	A	10	10	4	4
	B	10	10	5	5
Chittoor	C	7	7	4	4
	D	6	6	3	3
Kurnool	E	10	10	7	7
	F	10	10	7	7
Cuddapah	G	5	5	4	4
	H	7	7	4	4
Total		**8**	**8**	**5**	**5**

Source: Field data.

Note:
1. Total Mandays generated.
2. Total Male days.
3. Total Hired days.
4. Total hired Male days.

Table—5.1 shows a clear picture of the mean values of mandays generated in each sample village. Ploughing, being an activity to be take up only by male members the involvement of female labour is not seen in this activity. On an average per crop, per acre in Anantapur district total mandays generated was ten days in each village out of which, four mandays are hired days in Rachanapalli village and five hired days in Kotnur village. The generation of mandays is low in Cuddapah district i.e. only five mandays per crop, per acre for ploughing. The involvement of hired mandays was also low.

In the Table—5.1, for analysis purpose village-wise statistics have been taken into consideration. As per our sample there are eight villages in total at the rate of two villages selected from two different mandals of each district. For convenience purpose the names of the villages are shown with the help of alphabets, where A,B denote to Rachanapalli and Kotnur of Anantapur and Hindupur Mandals respectively, C,D denote to Gangundrapalli and Baripalli villages of Chandragiri and Palamaneru mandals, E,F, denote to Karivena and Jalimanchi villages of Atmakur and Emmiganur mandals and Kuruvapalli and Ganganapalli denote to Rayachoti and LakkiReddipalli mandals of Anantapur, Chittoor, Kurnool and Cuddapah districts respectively.

Levelling

Levelling is an activity is which the operations like making ridges and furrows is involved. After ploughing of the land is completed usually the farmers takeup this levelling activity to prepare the soil for plantation of saplings. The involvement of female labour is less in this activity. In our sample the number of total mandays generated, the number of male and female days and hired labour days is collected and presented in Table—5.2.

Table—5.2 Average mandays generated in Levelling activity

(in Mandays)

District	*Village*	1	2	3	4	5	6
Anantapur	A	10.00	10.00	–	4.00	4.00	–
	B	9.00	9.00	–	5.00	5.00	–
Chittoor	C	8.00	5.00	3.00	–	–	–
	D	8.00	5.00	3.00	4.00	2.00	2.00
Kurnool	E	10.00	5.00	5.00	6.00	2.00	4.00
	F	13.00	9.00	4.00	6.00	3.00	3.00
Cuddapah	G	7.00	4.00	3.00	4.00	2.00	2.00
	H	8.00	8.00	–	4.00	4.00	–
	Total	**9.00**	**7.00**	**2.00**	**4.00**	**3**	**1**

Source: Field data.

Note:
1. Total mandays generated.
2. Male days generated.
3. Female days generated.
4. Total Hired days generated.
5. Hired male days generated.
6. Hired female days generated.

It is evident from Table—5.2 that in Anantapur district in the two sample villages a total number of ten mandays are required to do the levelling work. Out of that four mandays are hired days. Female labour involvement is not seen in Anantapur district in levelling activity. In Chittoor, Kurnool and Cuddapah nearly three to 5 working days have been created for women in levelling activity. In these districts female labourers are also working on hired basis.

Weeding

Weeding is an important activity where a number of female labourers work in the farms. Weeding is done five to ten times during a year as sericulturists rear five crops per year. The involvement of labour is shown in Table—5.3.

Table—5.3 Average mandays generated in weeding activity

(in weeding)

District	*Village*	1	2	3	4	5
Anantapur	A	88.00	88.00	76.00	-	76.00
	B	98.00	98.00	78.00	-	78.00
Chittoor	C	72.00	72.00	56.00	-	56.00
	D	70.00	66.00	45.00	-	45.00
Kurnool	E	96.00	96.00	88.00	-	88.00
	F	88.00	88.00	83.00	-	83.00
Cuddapah	G	64.00	64.00	50.00	-	50.00
	H	57.00	57.00	46.00	-	46.00
Total		**79.00**	**79.00**	**65.00**	-	**65.00**

Source: Field data.

Note:
1. Total mandays generated.
2. Total female days generated.
3. Total hired days generated.
4. Total hired male days.
5. Total hired female days generated.

It is clear from the Table–5.3 that in the weeding activity the total number of working days generated are high in Anantapur district followed by Kurnool and Chittoor districts. In all the sample districts the weeding work has been done by female labour force and nearly 80 per cent of them are hired labourers.

Farm yard Manure Application

Farm yard manure application is another important activity usually taken up by the sericulturist during the cultivation of mulberry crop one time in a year. Though the sericulturist grows mulberry for five times during a year, he she applies Farmyard Manure (FYM) only once in a year. The generation of mandays during this activity is shown in Table–5.4.

Table—5.4 shows a clear picture of the mean values of the working days generated in Farm Yard Manure application. FYM application is taking nearly 12 days to 17 days in both the villages in Anantapur district. Out of this seven days are hired days. The female labour involvement is also high ranging from a minimum of 3 days to a maximum of 10 days in the sample area. Usually farmers engage hired labour for FYM application. Therefore hired labour days and both male and females are also high.

Table—5.4 Average mandays generated in FYM application

District	*Village*	1	2	3	4	5	6
Anantapur	A	17.00	6.00	11.00	7.00	3.00	4.00
	B	11.00	8.00	3.00	6.00	3.00	3.00
Chittoor	C	11.00	7.00	4.00	5.00	3.00	2.00
	D	13.00	8.00	5.00	7.00	4.00	3.00
Kurnool	E	9.00	2.00	7.00	7.00	–	7.00
	F	9.00	6.00	3.00	4.00	2.00	2.00
Cuddapah	G	8.00	5.00	3.00	4.00	2.00	2.00
	H	10.00	6.00	4.00	4.00	2.00	2.00
Total		**12.00**	**7.00**	**5.00**	**6.00**	**3.00**	**3.00**

Source: Field data.

Note:
1. Total mandays generated.
2. Total male days generated.
3. Total female days generated.
4. Total Hired days generated.
5. Total Hired male days generated.
6. Total Hired female days generated.

Chemical Manure Application

Now-a-days chemical manures have become compulsory for getting high yields of the crops. The chemical manures are applied for five times during a year. For every crop the application of chemical manures is necessary. So that the frequency per year in the case of mulberry crop is usually four to five times. In our sample it is five times per annum as on an average all the farmers are cultivating mulberry for five times during a year. Table—5.5 shows about the generation of mandays through this activity.

Table—5.5 Average mandays generated in chemical manure application

District	*Village*	*1*	*2*	*3*	*4*
Anantapur	A	10.00	10.00	2.00	2.00
	B	10.00	10.00	4.00	4.00
Chittoor	C	8.00	8.00	3.00	3.00
	D	5.00	5.00	4.00	4.00
Kurnool	E	9.00	9.00	5.00	5.00
	F	8.00	8.00	–	–
Cuddapah	G	8.00	8.00	2.00	2.00
	H	8.00	8.00	2.00	2.00
Total		**8.00**	**8.00**	**3.00**	**3.00**

Source: Field data.

Note: 1. Total mandays generated.

2. Total male days generated.

3. Total Hired days generated.

4. Total male hired days generated.

It is evident from Table—5.5 that on an average Five to Seven working days have been generated per activity per acre through chemical manure application. It is interesting to note that the involvement of female labour is not at all seen anywhere in the chemical manure application in any sample village. Usually chemical manures are applied only by male labourers. Therefore the female labour participation is not there in chemical manure application.

Silkworm Rearing

As mentioned in the earlier chapters, silkworm rearing is a very delicate activity to be carried over with utmost care at each phase of its process right from chawkie rearing to cocoon harvesting. It requires lot of patience, skill and time. Usually in sericulture activity, this part of operation is generally carried over by women in more numbers. In the following pages the working days generated in the five different phases (five Instars) of rearing 200-250 dfls is presented.

It is clear from the Table—5.6 that out of a mean value of 10 mandays generated, during I instar there was no involvement of female labourers. All the work generated was looked after by the own labour that too only male labour during the earlier stages of silkworm rearing. Only in Kurnool district in one village five hired mandays were generated in our sample. Table—5.7 gives a clear picture of II instar.

Table—5.6 Average mandays generated during I instar

District	*Village*	*1*	*2*	*3*	*4*
Anantapur	A	10.00	-	10.00	10.00
	B	13.00	-	13.00	13.00
Chittoor	C	8.00	-	8.00	8.00
	D	8.00	-	8.00	8.00
Kurnool	E	11.00	5.00	6.00	11.00
	F	10.00	-	10.00	11.00
Cuddapah	G	8.00	-	8.00	8.00
	H	7.00	-	7.00	7.00
Total		8.00	-	8.00	8.00

Source: Field data.

Note: 1. Total Mandays generated.

2. Hired Mandays generated.

3. Own Mandays generated.

4. Male days generated.

Table—5.7 Average man days generated during II instar

District	Village	1	2	3	4	5
Anantapur	A	12.00	4.00	8.00	8.00	4.00
	B	12.00	3.00	9.00	7.00	5.00
Chittoor	C	11.00	–	11.00	11.00	–
	D	9.00	–	9.00	9.00	–
Kurnool	E	10.00	5.00	5.00	9.00	1.00
	F	12.00	4.00	8.00	8.00	4.00
Cuddapah	G	8.00	–	8.00	8.00	–
	H	7.00	–	7.00	7.00	–
Total		**10.00**	**4.00**	**6.00**	**6.00**	**4.00**

Source: Field data.

Note:
1. Total Mandays generated.
2. Total hired days generated.
3. Total own days generated.
4. Total Male days generated.
5. Total female days generated.

It is clear from Table—5.7 that during the II instar on an average seven to 12 mandays have been generated in all the sample villages. The involvement of female labour is not there in our sample in Cuddapah and Chittoor districts. In the other two districts females labourers also participated actively in this work. Out of 12 mandays generated only 3 to 5 days are hired days and the remaining are own labour days. Female family labourers also had equal participation in rearing silkworms during this stage. In Table—5.8 average man days generated in III instar is presented.

Table—5.8 Average mandays generated during III instar

District	Village	1	2	3	4	5
Anantapur	A	19.00	5.00	14.00	10.00	9.00
	B	23.00	12.00	11.00	16.00	7.00
Chittoor	C	17.00	10.00	7.00	7.00	10.00
	D	15.00	8.00	7.00	9.00	6.00
Kurnool	E	15.00	5.00	12.00	11.00	4.00
	F	18.00	7.00	11.00	13.00	5.00
Cuddapah	G	15.00	5.00	10.00	10.00	5.00
	H	12.00	5.00	7.00	7.00	5.00
Total		**16.00**	**6.00**	**10.00**	**10.00**	**6.00**

Source: Field data.

Note: 1. Mandays generated.

2. Hired days generated.

3. Own days generated.

4. Male days generated.

5. Female days generated.

It is evident from Table—5.8 that the involvement of family labour is high even in III instar. Apart from family labour some hired labour was also taken for assistance. As silkworms grow larger and larger in size the attention shown towards them also increases. Feeding has to be done at regular intervals and silkworms are to be protected from the attract of pests and diseases. On an average 23 working days to 12 working days have been generated during this III instar in the sample villages.

Table—5.9 Average man days generated during IV instar

District	*Village*	*1*	*2*	*3*	*4*	*5*
Anantapur	A	32.00	7.00	25.00	25.00	7.00
	B	33.00	22.00	11.00	22.00	11.00
Chittoor	C	30.00	22.00	8.00	8.00	20.00
	D	31.00	21.00	10.00	20.00	11.00
Kurnool	E	27.00	8.00	19.00	21.00	6.00
	F	28.00	7.00	21.00	22.00	6.00
Cuddapah	G	29.00	15.00	14.00	10.00	19.00
	H	30.00	20.00	10.00	14.00	16.00
	Total	**30.00**	**15.00**	**15.00**	**18.00**	**12.00**

Source: Field data.

Note: 1. Total Mandays generated.
2. Total hired days generated.
3. Total own days generated.
4. Total Male days generated.
5. Total Female days generated.

Table—5.9 gives a clear picture of employment generation during IV instar. On an average 27 mandays to 33 mandays generated during this IV instar of rearing of silkworms. As the number of mandays increasing in each instar, the involvement of hired labour is also increasing. Female labour participation ranges between six to twenty working days in different villages.

Table—5.10 Average man days generated during V instar

District	*Village*	*1*	*2*	*3*	*4*	*5*
Anantapur	A	159.00	67.00	92.00	51.00	100.00
	B	157.00	69.0	88.00	61.00	95.00
Chittoor	C	159.00	71.00	88.00	57.00	102.00
	D	159.00	70.00	89.00	72.00	87.00
Kurnool	E	159.00	59.00	90.00	61.00	88.00
	F	170.00	72.00	98.00	68.00	102.00
Cuddapah	G	160.00	70.00	90.00	60.00	100.00
	H	156.00	67.00	89.00	59.00	97.00
	Total	**158.00**	**68.00**	**90.00**	**60.00**	**98.00**

Source: Field data.

Note:
1. Total mandays generated.
2. Total hired days generated.
3. Total own days generated.
4. Total male days generated.
5. Total female days generated.

It is clear from Table—5.10 that on an average 158 mandays have been generated during V instar. This is ranging between 149 to 170 mandays in our sample villages. The hired days comprise of 52 per cent out of the total mandays generated in this sample. The involvement of female labour was very high i.e. around 98 days on an average and ranging between 103 to 88 female labour days. During the cocoon harvesting season i.e. during the last three days of the silkworm rearing activity the involvement of labour requirement will be very high. It is interesting to note that female labour participation is very high in this instar when compared other instars.

Therefore one hectare of irrigated mulberry garden created working days ranging from 3,113 to 4,225 in our study area. Out of which female labour involvement was from 1,900 working days to 2,562 working days. This ranges between 45 per cent to 61 per cent of total labour days generated through sericulture activity.

Table—5.11 gives a detailed picture of mandays generated from both mulberry cultivation and silkworm rearing (200 to 250 dfls) per acre per crop. The average mandays created in each activity are taken for calculating the total mandays.

Table—5.11 Average mandays generated per crop per acre

(in mandays)

	A Mulberry cultivation	*OWN*	*Hired*	*Male*		*Female*		*Total*
				Own	*Hired*	*Own*	*Hired*	
1.	Ploughing	3	5	3	5	–	–	8
2.	Levelling	5	4	4	3	1	1	9
3.	Weeding	14	65	–	–	14	65	79
4.	FYM application	5	7	4	4	1	4	12
5.	Chemical Manure application	5	3	5	3	–	–	8
	Total	**32**	**84**	**16**	**15**	**16**	**69**	**116**
B.	**Silkworm Rearing**	Own	Hired	Male		Female		Total
6.	I Instar	8	–	8		–		8
7.	II Instar	6	4	6		4		10
8.	III Instar	10	6	10		6		16
9.	IV Instar	15	15	18		12		30
10.	V Instar	90	68	60		98		158
	Grand total	129	93	102		120		222
				133		205		338

Source: Field data.

The involvement of family labour is gradually reducing in the study area. This is because of the improved standard of living of farmers as a result of sericulture practice for more than six years.

Conclusion

Sericulture as already mentioned, generates a chain of economic activities providing employment to the people in rural, urban and semi-urban areas. Through Sericulture, the incidence of unemployment, disguised unemployment and seasonal unemployment is relieved to a great extent. Specially in the agricultural sector, the human labour involvement in the various activities of silkworm rearing is high when compared to mulberry cultivation. Further the involvement of female labour is present both in mulberry cultivation and silkworm rearing. Silkworm rearing provides high employment opportunities to both hired and female labour. Silkworm rearing is a peculiar activity can be done more efficiently by women.

6

Problems of Sericulture

The study of sericulture development in the Rayalaseema districts, presented in the preceding chapters, shows that sericulture has made quick and remarkable progress during the past 15 years, as small and marginal farmers in this area are being attracted more and more to this activity because of the prospects it holds. Being agro-based, it has vast potential for generating income and employment opportunities primarily to the rural masses. This potential to have further increased with governmental intervention to promote and achieve an all round development of sericulture with the help of Five-Year Programme Financed by the World Bank.

There is, no doubt, that an increase in the production of cocoons relieved the silk industry from the problem of scarcity of raw material. But the farmer who grows mulberry and rears silkworms faces certain other problems in the operation of sericulture activity. Unless these problems are identified and necessary action taken, the programme of planned sericulture development may not succeed and the targeted growth can not be achieved. This chapter attempts to highlight the factors which come in the way of sericulture development in the sample districts.

Problems of Sericulture

The sericulture industry has been suffering from many problems pertaining to its organisation, marketing, finance, technology and extension. Depending on the intensity of the problems encountered by the sample sericulturists, their perceptions are collected, and presented in the following pages.

Intensity of Pests and Diseases for Silkworms

Mulberry cultivation, the first step in producing silk is an easy job and does not involve any special techniques or required special skills or knowledge. Mulberry is affected very rarely by leaf rust or leaf spot diseases. Though there are some measures to control pests, the only measure followed by the sample sericulturists is sparing the pest affected leaves from plant and destroying them.

The major operation of sericulturists is silkworm rearing which needs particular care and attention of rearers. It is the most delicate activity in entire operation of silk production.

Grassarie, Flacheric, pebrine and uzyfly are the enemies of silkworms and silkworm rearers, which decrease quality and quantity of cocoons therefore as a precautionary measure, silkworm rearers have to use nylon nets and have the rearing equipment properly cleaned with formaline and also use Uzycide and 'Reshamkeet Oushad' as preventive measures. Once the silkworms are attacked by Grasserie, Flacherie or Uzyfly, infected silkworms should be destroyed at once. There are no control measures to prevent these diseases except conducting rearing operation under most hygienic conditions.

Since frequent occurrence of diseases to silkworms is one of the major problems troubling sericulture some new farmers who want to adopt sericulture are scared of these pests and diseases hesite to take it up. So, research organisations are seized of this problem, and are trying seriously to find a remedy for it. If a satisfactory remedy is not found at an early date the yield of good cocoons will gradually decrease on one hand and on the other hand the prospects of sericulture development would receive a setback.

Non-availability of Layings

Sericulturists generally buy layings (CBDFLS) from government grainages and licensed seed-producers. The layings would be available adequately round the year except in the summer season. Some times inadequacy, instability and poor quality of CBDFLS exposes sericulturists to some real trouble and lead to under-utilization of the available mulberry leaf. In such a situation sericulture becomes less economical. Some of the sample farmers express the opinion that disease free layings are very often affected by diseases.

The non-availability of layings is one of the major problems faced by the sericulturists in Anantapur. The existing grainage facilities are inadequate and often fail to meet the demand. Normally, for every 405 hectares, there should be one grainage with a production capacity of ten lakh layings per year. Though 42,789 hectares (1998-99) of land are under mulberry cultivation in Anantapur, there are only six grainages, grossly inadequate to meet the legitimate demands of sericulturist. Therefore the sericulturists obtain layings, either from the near-by Karnataka state or from private grainages. To remedy the situation and to meet the growing demand, grainages for Local and Foreign races have also to be increased. Further the government has to take necessary steps to introduce bivoltine layings for commercial rearing in this district. The same problem is prevailing even in the other districts of Rayalaseema Region.

Fluctuations in Cocoon Prices

Steady and speedy growth of any economic activity would not be possible without a stable and minimum economic price for its products. This statement is particularly applicable to the sericulture industry. There are violent fluctuations in the prices of its different products. These fluctuations are mainly due to a lack of guarantee of cocoon crop, wide variations in the quality of cocoons produced, absence of standardisation and quality control, poor and inadequate marketing facilities, and finally import of silk from other countries. During the rainy season, the quality of cocoons is likely to be poor though the yield may be higher. As a consequence the supply of cocoons in the market would be in excess causing a fall in the price of cocoons. During the survey conducted for the present study it is found that the price of cocoons fluctuated from Rs. 80 to Rs. 140 per kilogram of cocoons.

Moreover, sericulturist are forced to sell their cocoons at the prevailing price, because once the moth emerges out of the cocoon the cocoons become useless for reeling. As the sericulturist are forced to sell the cocoons within that time at the price prevailing in the market, their income suffers. In addition to this, the reelers also have the obligation to undertake the reeling work immediately.

To obviate these pressures stifling units can be established by the government or private entrepreneurs or both, so that the cocoons may be steam-stifled making the worm die in the cocoon. Thus, the cocoon can be preserved for a long time extending over months. Such of processing and preserving helps the sericulturist to realise better prices. The stifling technique facilitates the creation of buffer stocks of cocoons so as to maintain price stability. Therefore, steps have to be taken to develop the necessary infrastructure for stifling and building buffer stocks.

Further, the increase in the output of cocoons and raw silk should not be allowed to affect the price of cocoons through the manipulation by middle men. Fixation of cocoon and raw silk floor price is an essential ingredient of a package policy necessary to sustain the growth of sericulture.

Shortage of Labour

Mulberry cultivation does not require any technical knowledge or special skills. Hence, ordinary agricultural labourers with simple skills are enough for this activity. Mulberry cultivation and silkworm rearing creates profitable employment opportunities to the farmers. In spite of its employment potential, mulberry growers are suffering from shortage of labour. It is probably because mulberry can be cultivated even in small segments of land holdings. Hence, agricultural labourers who own less than one acre are also cultivating mulberry and silkworm rearing, thereby creating labour shortage for small as well as big farmers. Sericulture has been inducing not only small and marginal farmers but also agricultural labourers to take up self employment. The labour shortage in cultivating mulberry can be overcome by introducing appropriate machinery in the mulberry fields on co-operative basis.

Climatic Disturbances

Cool climatic throughout the year is a prerequisite for silkworm rearing, cocoon production and high renditta. Climatic disturbances upset cocoon production. In the tropical climate especially during summer sericulturists are advised to use air coolers, drip water on the rearing sheds, arrange the rearing rooms under the shade of the big trees etc., to overcome the adverse effects of hot summer. The adoption of these new techniques though expensive marginally, reduces the adverse effects on the quantity and quality of cocoons and income per acre of the mulberry garden. High leaf yield from the mulberry garden raised on good soil which has good irrigation facilities may compensate the higher cost arising out of the extremes of summer climate. In any case climatic hazards do add to the drudgery of silkworms rearing necessitating greater care and attention on the part of sericulturists.

Other things being equal, the fact remain that a hot climate is a deterrent for sericulture entrepreneurship. As sericulture is a labour intensive enterprise, high wages that prevail in the agricultural growth centres also constitute an obstacle for sericulture expansion. Big farmers though they face better capacity to face the climatic hazards, may not like the increased managerial responsibility and time required to look after sericulture. In contrast small farmers lack the resources to provide adequate facilities to counteract the hazards of severe heat during summer for silkworm rearing.

Shortage of Skilled Workers

Crops other than sericulture may not need special skills and techniques. But it is the peculiar characteristic of sericulture activity that it require skilled workers, and the need for them is high during the period of silkworm rearing. As mentioned earlier, silkworm rearing is a very delicate activity which needs much care and attention as silkworms at the infant stages look like ants. Tender mulberry leaves have to be cut into very fine pieces and spread on the silkworms. Generally silkworms take 25 to 28 days for obtaining complete growth and be ready to spin cocoon . During this period they undergo several changes and are very easily prone to diseases. Skilled labour is very much essential during this period to maintain timely feeding with required quantity and quality of leaves and also protect them against infecting diseases.

As sericulture is developing and progressing in all the study districts, steps should be taken to enhance the number of skilled workers and make them available. Training should be given to those interested in taking up sericulture and also the agricultural labour in the required skills at the district and block level centres. It, undoubtedly, would increase the yield of cocoons and reduce, unemployment among the rural population.

Inadequate Finance for Investment

The average sericulturist is either a small or a marginal farmer with limited means who requires financial assistance. As we know, the capital requirements for cultivating one acre of mulberry and silkworm rearing are definitely more than any other commercial or food crop. Therefore there is the need to assure adequate finance for making the required investment in sericulture. It is time that sericulturists have obtained from time to time institutional loans from commercial banks and cooperatives. But the amount received by them is far from adequate to meet their needs. Therefore, they have to borrow from other sources like friends, relatives and moneylenders at high rates of interest. Another problem regarding financial assistance is that the financial institutions are much too conservative to extend loans readily to sericulturists. Hence, for an orderly development of sericulture, institutional agencies should identify the special features and needs of sericulturists and the extent of finance required for fixed and working capital. Unless the institutional finance is streamlined the potentialities of sericulture may not be realised fully.

Shortage of Rearing Equipment

The equipment required for silkworm rearing is of a special kind. While it is supremely important in sericulture activity, it can not be used for any other purpose. Since to possess the equipment needs considerable initial investment, only a few farmers can afford to procure it. Although banks and co-operatives are extending credit for this purpose, the amount sanctioned by them for obtaining rearing equipment including shed is inadequate. Hence, majority of the silkworm rearers are hiring chandriakas and other equipment according to their necessity. Therefore, the State Government may help the sericulturists to supply them at subsidised rates.

Inadequate Market Facilities

Marketing facilities are inadequate in the Cuddapah and Kurnool districts whereas in the Anantapur and Chittoor districts the problem is not felt. Absence of proper marketing facilities constitutes a major obstacle for the orderly and rapid development of sericulture. Sericulturists of Anantapur are sending the cocoons mostly to the Karnataka markets. In the Karnataka regulated markets, the prevailing practice is that cocoons are purchased by dealers in an open auction after a visual examination of the lots. Due regard to the quality of cocoons is not paid anywhere. The problems which sericulturists are facing in the Karnataka markets are mostly in the form of loss of sample cocoons supplied to the brokers, absence of proper weighing and unjustifiable deduction of certain percentage on the pretext that the produce is of inferior quality. Moreover, the market costs vary from place to place depending on distance and problems of transport.

At present there are six markets in the district of Anantapur, at Kadiri, Hindupur, Dharmavaram, Madakasira, Penukonda and Anantapur. Sericulturists from the other mandals of the district have to travel a long way to bring their cocoons to these markets facing the difficulties of transportation, physical strain etc., Some of the rearers however take the cocoons to the Ramanagara, Vijayapura, Kanakapura and Sidlaghatta markets in Karanataka to get fair price. So, an efficient marketing organisation either through regulated markets or private dealers has to be set up giving it the top most priority. Appropriate infrastructure has to be built up with the creation of marketing facilities in the proximity of farmers so as to economise the cost of cocoon transportation. Moreover, efficient marketing organisation may help in arresting wide fluctuations in the price of cocoons by stabilising the market trends. sufficient number of local markets may stimulate reeling activity and thereby promote silk industry in the districts and thus generate more income and more employment.

Securing Extension Officers Advice

As sericulture is not a routine type of activity, it requires constant improvement based on research results conducted by research agencies such as the central sericultural Research and Training Institute, Mysore and other. When the growth of sericulture is accelerated, more and more new sericulturists who joined the enterprise need scientific information, skill and knowledge regarding all aspects of it, including raising the mulberry garden and rearing silkworms. The field officers concerned are required to pay frequent visits to the sericulturists to guide them in their work, to check the spread of diseases as and when they are detected, to direct the farmers to cultivate better varieties of mulberry with proper application of manure, fertilizer and watering and to make them adopt cross breed races of silk worms and better methods of rearing. If the new sericulturists fail to utilise these extension services properly they would naturally fail in their new enterprises. Their failure, partial or full, may discourage other farmers and upset the process of innovation in introducing the new enterprise. Speedy growth of sericulture postulates intensive extension services to facilities healthy innovation.

In any case, speedy growth of sericulture, involving innovations on the part of the farmers will not be feasible without the establishment of a competent extension service department which has to enlighten and advice sericulturists. So the government has to build up a competent extension cadre to assist sericulture farmers.

Problems of Women Sericulturists

In the earlier pages the problems of sericulture in general pertaining to the activities like, management, establishment, labour shortage, financial assistance marketing etc are discussed. Women's role in the activities of sericulture is there since the beginning of the activities. But in the present study apart from all the general problems, women sericulturists face particular problems with regard to marketing of cocoons, transportation, availability of market information, interference of middle men etc. Being uneducated women sericulturists without any male person's support unable to go to market due to a number of reasons. They are very easily prone to be exploited by the middle men. Therefore proper marketing and transport facilities can be arranged to make more women to take active roles in sericulture. Single woman sericulturists have to depend on others for marketing their cocoons.

Conclusion

Though sericulture in the Rayalaseema region is leading towards prosperity, but the problems faced by the sericulturists hinder the progress of sericulture. New farmers may hesitate to take up this activity because of these problems. Hence, the government should be requested through the cooperatives to pay due attention to solve them, otherwise, it will affect the growth of sericulture and those who are already engaged in sericulture activity may withdraw from it. Special attention should be given to solve the problem of women in sericulture to raise their active participation.

7

Summary and Conclusions

Developing countries like India have still to rely very largely on the agriculture sector for economic development, which has occupied a vital place in the development strategies of India. However in recent years Indian agriculture is on the threshold of a stage of development characterised by a shift from static technology to modern technology.

In this context sericulture, with its vast potential for income and employment generation in rural areas, plays an important role in alleviating poverty. It is one of the crop enterprises which is identified as one of the most appropriate labour intensive cottage industries. This activity combines both agriculture and industry. Sericulture for example, has the credit of taking our tradition bound agriculture into a modernised agriculture by intensive use of land, labour and capital.

Sericulture is best suited to a country like India where manpower and land resources are in surplus. It generates direct and indirect employment in various ways. By creating more employment opportunities in rural, urban and semi-urban areas, it not only arrests rural migration but also promotes a series of cottage and small scale industries. 'Silk', the final product of the sericulture enterprise, has very good associations with the customs and traditions of the people living all over the world. Further, with improvement in the economic conditions of the people, the demand for silk is also increasing within the country and abroad.

Sericulture in India has a very long history. It is as old as Indian civilization. It has passed through a number of phases, rise and fall, in its long journey towards prosperity. During the last 20 years India has made tremendous progress in the production of mulberry silk for which there is an increasing international demand. Recently, sericulture in India has achieved enormous changes and progress by evolving suitable mulberry varieties, silkworm races and techniques suitable for the tropical climatic conditions. With the evolution and introduction of more productive silkworm races, productivity has increased and sericulture has become a highly remunerative activity.

More and more farmers in India have taken up sericulture activity and the industry which was once confined to five states only has spread to almost all states of India. Andhra Pradesh though not a traditional state in silk production, occupies second place in the country in producing mulberry raw silk. In Andhra Pradesh, Rayalaseema Region is showing enormous growth potential in sericulture, which in turn has improved the economic standards of their rural population. This has proved as the most suitable activity in providing gainful employment opportunities to both males and females. Especially it has been identified as an activity suitable for women, aged and children. Without going to farm women can themselves engage profitably in this sericulture activity.

In this context analytical and empirical investigations carried out in the four Rayalaseema districts reveal several interesting factor which have been presented in the preceding chapters in detail. Here an attempt is made to put together all these observations, so as to present an overall view of the results emerging from the present study.

The main objective of the study is to examine the growth of sericulture in Rayalaseema Region and its role in the generation of employment for rural women in this region. As it is not possible to cover the entire region, to keep the study within manageable limits without affecting adversely the investigation, two mandals from each district i.e., Anantapur and Hindupur from Anantapur district, Chandragiri and Atmakur from Chittoor district, Atmakur and Emmiganur from Kurnool district and Rayachoti and Lakki Reddy palli from Cuddapah districts are selected. Again eight villages at the rate of one from each mandal have been selected for the analysis of economics of sericulture in general and the creation of employment opportunities for women in particular.

To meet the above main objectives hypotheses were formulated to test whether 1. Sericulture is providing stable income and employment to many rural agricultural families and a livelihood to scores of landless farm and non-farm women labourers giving much economic strength. 2. The role of women in the process of sericulture development has increased as employment generation for women is more than men in mulberry cultivation, silkworm rearing and 3. The benefits of sericulture are not fully reaching the family for the socio-economic upliftment as the women are not involved in marketing and financial transactions. The primary data was collected with the help of a schedule and the collected data has been analysed using SPSS 10.0. The specific tools used are cross tabulations, percentages, mean, growth analysis, fitting of trend lines etc.

Historically China is the motherland of silk. Chinese treasured the secret of Silk for centuries together, but gradually it spread to Japan, Korea, India and other parts of the world. India ranks next to China in production of mulberry rawsilk.

Sericulture in India is broadly classified into two distinct sectors namely mulberry and non-mulberry. Though India has the unique distinction of being the only country in the world which produces all the four commercially known varieties of silk, over 90 per cent of the silk produced in India is mulberry silk. Production of mulberry rawsilk in the country is mainly confined to the states of Karnataka, Andhra Pradesh, West Bengal, Tamil Nadu and Jammu and Kashmir. With the liberal financial allocation in the Five year plans and the contribution of the Sericulture Department through its research, this activity has proved to be an effective tool for eradication of rural poverty and unemployment.

Andhra Pradesh state has developed as second state in India in mulberry raw silk production after Karnataka. The area under mulberry crop which was only 74.31 thousand hectares in 1990-91 has increased to 116.18 thousand hectares in 1998-99 in Andhra

Pradesh, showing a linear growth rate of 5.4439 per cent. The cocoon production and raw silk production have raised significantly for last two decades. But infrastructural facilities have not grown commensurately to meet the increasing demands of this industry in the state.

The National Sericulture Project and many other projects which are under implementation in the state are also responsible for the commendable growth of sericulture.

The districts of Anantapur and Chittoor are adjacent to Karnataka state. Apart from this all the districts in Rayalaseema Region are drought prone. Inspite of severe drought conditions, there is enormous growth of mulberry during the last 20 years.

Sericulture has become a most promising activity for the farmers in these Rayalaseema Region. In Anantapur the area under mulberry increased from 29, 861 to 42, 789 thousand hectares and cocoon production increased from 147.37 to 155.69 lakh kgs during the period from 1990-91 to 1998-99. In other districts also there is an encouraging trend with regard to mulberry cultivation, silkworm rearing and raw silk production. The area under mulberry has increased from 15,198, and 25,251, 6,348, to 8,754, 6,141, to 8,178 hectares in Chittoor, Kurnool and Cuddapah districts. The infrastructural facilities available in these districts have also helped for the fast growth of sericulture. But still there is a need to improve infrastructural facilities to meet the growing demand of sericulture.

Mulberry is cultivated in the sample villages Rachanapalli and Kotnur , of Anantapur district Ganganapalli and Barripalli of Chittoor district Karivena and Jalimanchi of Kurnool district Kuruvapalli and Ganganapalli of Cuddapah district under irrigated conditions. The source for irrigation is through bore wells and dug wells. The concentration of mulberry is high around 200 to 300 acres in each villages. There are 100 to 150 sericulturists in each village. The sample farmers were drawn at random at the rate of 30 farmers from each village making the total sample 240. Thus the study covered 60 sample sericulturists from each district.

Of the 240 sample farmers 32 are marginal farmers with less than one acre land holdings. 73 are small farmers and 135 are big farmers. The average size of land holdings of these categories of farmers is 1.78 acres, 4.22 acres and 12.93 acres. Of the total sample 69 farmers (29 per cent) belong to the SC/ST, 63 belong to (26 per cent) BC community and 108 belong to (45 per cent) OC community. Regarding the literary levels of the farmers 134 (55.8 per cent) are illiterates 102 (42.6 per cent) have school education 4(1.6per cent) have collegiate education.

The cropping pattern reveals that, apart from paddy, groundnut in Anantapur district, Jawan in Kurnool district, Ragi and groundnut in Chittoor and Cuddapah districts dominate other crops. The main source of income for the sample households is agriculture.

Women occupy nearly 50 per cent of the total population in these districts. Nearly 70 per cent of women depend on agriculture as agricultural labourers for their livelihood. The literacy rate among women is very low even below the state general literacy rate.

Though all the Rayalaseema districts are subject to frequent droughts, the area under mulberry in them has increased year after year because the plant is drought resistant and gives more income in shorter intervals. A number of variables which focus on the structure of costs and returns among the sample households with different sizes of mulberry land holdings have been examined.

The majority of sample households have adopted sericulture for more than six(6) years in all the sample districts. Most of the mulberry land holdings are below one acre and one to two acres. Mulberry land holdings, which are more than two acres are only a few. Hence, one hectare becomes a large unit and therefore one acre is adopted as the unit for analysing the variables that influence the sericulture practice. There are 26 sericulturists with less than one acre area 32 have between one to two acres and the remaining two farmers cultivate mulberry in a garden of more than two acres each in Anantapur district. Similarly, in Chittoor district 50 sericulturists cultivate mulberry in less than one acre 10 have between one to two acres. In Kurnool and Cuddapah districts there are 27 and 41, sericulturists in the category of less than one acre mulberry area, 32 and 19 Sericulturists have between one and two acres and one in Kurnool district cultivate mulberry in more than two acres of mulberry land.

As mulberry is a perennial crop, the initial establishment of the garden is of crucial importance and no compromises can be made on the initial establishment. The profitability of sericulture largely depends on the production of mulberry leaf and its conversion into quality cocoons at economic costs. The garden once established yields for about 12 to 15 years. The mulberry plantation is made with cuttings according to the row system which is popularly called the 'Kolar system'. Both the local and Kanvaz varieties (M5) are used by the sample sericulturists. The estimated cost of initial establishment of one acre irrigated mulberry garden is around Rs. 7,650 in Anantapur district, Rs. 7, 540 , in Chittoor district and Rs. 7,340 in Kurnool district and Rs. 7,580 in Cuddapah district. The management cost of this garden during the establishment year is estimated to the Rs. 7,250, Rs. 7,250, Rs. 6,750, Rs.6,760 in Anantapur, Chittoor, Kurnool and Cuddapah districts, respectively.

Once the mulberry garden is established it gives yield over a long period. The recurring expenditure involved in maintenance of one acre of irrigated mulberry garden from the second year onwards is estimated as Rs. 13,330, Rs. 12,690, Rs.. 12,120 and Rs. 12,280 in Anantapur, Chittoor, Kurnool and Cuddapah districts. With the involvement of family labour 30-40 per cent of this expenditure is reduced.

The mulberry leaf production per acre is of the order of 9,253 kgs in Anantapur district, 8,797 in Chittoor district, 8,250 in Kurnool district and 8,137 in Cuddapah district. The production cost of one kg. of mulberry leaf is Rs. 0.61, 0.67, 0.69, 0.70 in Anantapur, Chittoor, Kurnool and Cuddapah districts respectively. In the sample districts 128 Sericulturists (53.3) undertake the rearing activity in a separate shed in the dwelling houses. Rearing though in a separate shed, but when taken up in the dwelling house results frequently in infection to the silkworms. Therefore, a separate, well protected shed is essential to improve the quality and productivity of the cocoons.

The cost of investment on a rearing shed is around Rs. 30,000 and on rearing equipment is Rs.17,250 (for rearing 200-250 dfls). The quantity of silkworms reared depends on the size of the mulberry garden. The annual quantity of disease free layings reared per acre is around 250, 240, 230, 220, in Anantapur, Chittoor, Kurnool and Cuddapah districts. Generally all the sample sericulturists in the study area rear five crops in a year. On an average, the sample sericulturists rear 200 to 250 dfls per acre per crop. The estimated cost to rear 200 to 250 dfls is Rs. 10,505, Rs. 9,985, Rs. 10,025 and Rs.10,145 in Anantapur, Chittoor, Kurnool and Cuddapah districts respectively.

The rearing activity is labour intensive and accordingly the estimated expenditure on labour component is also more when compared to the other inputs involved in this activity. The involvement of family labour reduces the cost of rearing substantially. The total estimated cost of both mulberry cultivation and silkworm rearing is around Rs.16,155 in Anantapur district, Rs.15,880 in Chittoor district Rs.15,752 in Kurnool district and Rs.15,908 in Cuddapah district.

The involvement of family is a decisive factor in both mulberry cultivation and silkworm rearing to make the enterprise economical. The economics of sericulture depends on the successful rearing of silkworms and the cocoon yield. Failures of crops do occur due to diseases infecting silkworm resulting in crop losses. The average failure rate among the sample households works to be 20 to 25 per cent in the sample districts. It seems to be little bit alarming. To derive one kilogram of cocoons the leaf used should be around 30kg. Anything more than this reflects, the inefficient use of the leaf. The rearers in the study area have shown high efficiency. Particularly the rearers of Kurnool district have shown better efficiency with 24kg leaf per kg. of cocoons. The average cocoon yield is more or less the same in all the districts and it works out to be 41 kg per 100 dfls harvested.

The success of sericulture enterprise depends on the profits it beings. In the expenditure on mulberry cultivation and silkworm rearing, the cost involved in rearing silkworms is Rs. 10,505, Rs. 9,985 and Rs. 10,145 in the four Rayalaseema districts.

The average net returns per year from one acre of mulberry garden are of the order of Rs.30,045/- in Anantapur, Rs. 33,120/- in Chittoor Rs.37,448/- in Kurnool and Rs.30,712 in Cuddapah districts.

Training is an important aspect for the success of any activity. In the present sample among the 240 sample farmers 27, 42, 20, 14 Sericulturists have undergone training in the four districts of Rayalaseema namely Anantapur, Chittoor, Kurnool and Cuddapah respectively. Out of 240 sample farmers only 43 per cent have undergone training and with regard to financial assistance 128 Sericulturists (i.e. 53 per cent) have received loan and subsidies. Majority of the sample farmers expressed their willingness to undertake more area under mulberry cultivation.

With regard to the marketing of cocoons, sericulturists in the study area first prefer to take their cocoon products to the nearby local markets. Sericulturists in Anantapur and Chittoor districts usually go to Karnataka cocoon markets also. Sericulturists in the study area expressed that this occupation displaced crops like: paddy, jowar, wheat, ragi, sunflower and small millets.

Employment opportunities in sericulture can be categorised under two heads. Thus opportunities relating to mulberry cultivation and silkworm rearing which are agricultural in nature are undertaken in rural areas, and secondly those opportunities relating to silk reeling twisting, weaving and marketing which are undertaken mostly in semi-urban and urban areas. In this analysis the employment opportunities relating to the first category are studied.

It is well known that sericulture creates a chain of employment opportunities, both in rural, urban and semi-urban areas. Sericulture has wider employment potential for women also. Women can be involved in almost all the activities that generate from sericulture. There is a large Scope for women employment in this occupation. The working days generated in an acre of mulberry garden for males and females analysed in this present study. In one acre of mulberry garden and for rearing of 200-250 dfls on an average 338 mandays are generated, out of which 205 (61.5 per cent) are female working days. The study reveals that 3113 to 4725 working days have been generated in Anantapur, Chittoor, Kurnool and Cuddapah districts on an average. The mean values of the working days are taken for analysis.

The generation of employment opportunities for women in mulberry cultivation and silkworm rearing is more when compared to men. In the study area it ranges between 45 to 61 per cent in both mulberry cultivation and silkworm rearing. The involvement of family labour is 48 per cent and hired labour is 52 per cent. The involvement of family labour is below 50 per cent i.e. 42 per cent. This is because of the improved standard of living of farmers as a result of sericulture practice.

Apart from creation of gainful employment to women and aged people at homes, a number of indirect employment opportunities can also be created in the ancillary sectors of sericulture like manufacturing of rearing appliances, processing and spinning silk waste and in the extraction of pupae oil and pupae meal from the by-products of sericulture.

Thus the analysis clearly establishes the importance of sericulture over other crops in creation of employment opportunities production and net returns. It provides higher returns and gainful employment throughout the year relieving farmers, more particularly small and marginal farmers, from the clutches of disguised and seasonal unemployment. This enterprise makes ideal use of manpower water and land resources which are critical inputs in drought prone areas, where, the strategy of farm development should be the economic use of these inputs with a view to maximise returns.

In a growing enterprise like sericulture, the problems are bound to be many and unavoidable. But these problems should not impede the progress of this enterprise towards long range goals. The problems faced by sericulturists mainly relate to the diseases which infect silkworms, availability of layings shortage of labour, insufficient financial support from the government, climatic hazards, wide fluctuations in cocoon prices and also to some extent inadequacy of extension services. Women who involved in sericulture activity in the study area expressed that they have a little opportunities with regard to marketing of cocoons. Women being illiterate are not aware of the latest market information, fluctuations in the cocoon prices and for them transport also a major problem. therefore, though they involve fully in the activities from mulberry cultivation to silk cocoon production, the benefits reaching them, are not satisfactory. Women are not going to markets and dealing with financial transactions of cocoons.

Of these the most important are the diseases infecting silkworms, inadequate availability of layings, fluctuation in cocoon prices shortage of skilled labour, insufficient financial assistance and women not having access to deal with financial transactions.

To overcome the problems and to make this enterprise more attractive the following suggestions are made.

There is a need to introduce new varieties of mulberry, which have been found viable with regard to the quality and quantity of leaf by the research institutions.

The sericulturists must be encouraged to rear bivoltine variety of silkworm rather than multivoltine silkworms to obtain better income.

The average cocoon yield can be raised per 100 dfls by following proper techniques of silkworm rearing.

More farmers may be motivated to taken-up sericulture on a large scale through co-operative farming.

Irrigation facilities have to be bettered and enhanced by giving incentives to the farmers for digging wells.

Research Institutions should provide suitable and necessary knowledge to the potential farmers to over come the problems of pests and diseases.

To meet the growing demand for layings, adequate number of grainages should be opened and care must be taken to supply good quality of layings through them.

Stifling units can be established both by the government and private entrepreneurs to preserve the cocoons for longer periods to overcome the problem of fluctuations in cocoon prices. Labour shortage in cultivation of mulberry can be filled by introducing appropriate machinery on a co-operative basis which can be used by the sericulturists.

To reduce the intensity of summer, air coolers, dripping of water in sheds, arranging rearing rooms under tree shades hanging wet gunny bags on the doors and windows of rearing rooms and the use of sand beds many be employed.

Provision of training facilities to the labourers can solve the problem of shortage of skilled workers.

Special training programmes have to be arranged for women to make them to participate in more numbers. Training enhances their skill and thereby the silk production.

Middlemen interference must be reduced by establishing regulated markets in the nearby Mandal Headquarters.

Women have to be given awareness with regard to marketing of cocoons, their quality wise grading, weighing and other financial transactions.

Local women groups may be contacted and extension officers advices can be taken to motivate women to taken-up sericulture as a cottage industry to gain supportive income to their family and to raise their status in the society by becoming economically independent.

Mulberry silk has a very strong and expanding domestic and export market. It brings money from richer to the poorer sections as well as helps in earning valuable foreign exchange for the country. In Andhra Pradesh the scope for the development of sericulture is clear-cut in two directions. One relates to the expansion of sericulture in new areas and the other modernising the industry in the existing areas. There is a lot of scope for the development of sericulture in the southern Regions of Andhra Pradesh i.e., in Rayalaseema Region which needs to be given special attention in view of their climatic and natural advantages. Efforts have to be directed towards the improvement of mulberry varieties as well as silkworm races. A suitable variety of mulberry which is adoptable to the local environment and resistant to high temperature has to be developed.

Sericulture activity in India is basically individual farmers oriented. Hence, a comprehensive programme to cover the entire area in the district with the new practices should be drawn up.

Qualified and experienced staff should be deployed for extension work. Subsidies, incentives and awards should be given to progressive farmers especially women.

Apart from having separate rearing buildings and proper equipment for the maintenance of humidity and temperature, the farmers should also maintain hygienic conditions in the rearing areas. Training and extension centres have to be established at mandal levels to educate farmers especially women in reducing the incidence of diseases to silkworms and to get higher cocoon crops.

Further, as a predominant sector of rural development stability is the vital need of sericulture industry. Hence, efforts should be made to put the fortunes of this labour intensive activity on sound lines by establishing regional organisations for stabilising the silk prices. This step definitely ensures a fair price to the primary producer namely the silkworm rearer, at a level that would ensure stability and further promotion of mulberry cultivation and silkworm rearing. It also increases the involvement of women actively in this sericulture activity if there is price stability and timely availability of market information.

References

Books

Abdul Aziz & Hanumappa, H.C., Silk Industry—Problems and Prospects, Ashish Publishing House, New Delhi, 1985.

Acharya, J., Sericulture and Development, Development Sociology Series—1 Indian Publishers Distributors, Delhi, 1993.

Agarwal, S.K., & Others, Agricultural Economics and Co-operation, S. Chand & Co. Ltd., New Delhi, 1970.

Aruga Hisao, Principles of Sericulture, Oxford & IBH Publishing Co., (Pvt.) Ltd., New Delhi, 1994.

Bansal, P.C., Agricultural Problems of India, Oxford & IBH Publishing Company (Pvt.) Ltd., New Delhi, 1981.

——, Agriculture Situation in India—A Guide, Oxford & IBH Publishing Company, New Delhi, 1984.

Benerjee, P.K., Indian Agriculture Economy—Financing Small Farmers, Chetana Publications, New Delhi, 1977.

Benjamin, R.E., & Others, Economic of Agriculture, S. Chand & Co. Ltd., New Delhi, 1989.

Bepin, Behari, Rural Industrialisation in India, Vikas Publishing House, Ghaziabad, 1974.

Central Silk Board, Silk Man's Companion, Bangalore, 1989.

——, Silk Man's Companion, Bangalore, 1990.

——, Silk Man's Companion, Bangalore, 1992.

Central Sericultural Research & Training Institute., Achievements of CSRTI, Mysore.

——, Central Sericulture Research & Training Institute, Mysore Its Organisational Set Up, 1981.

Charsley, S.R., Culture and Sericulture Academic Press, New York, 1982.

Chowdhury, M.R., Indian Industries Development and Location, Fourth Edition, Oxford and IBH Publishing Co. (Pvt.) Ltd., New Delhi, 1970.

Dhar, P.N. & Lydall, H.F., The Role of Small Enterprises in Indian Economic Development, Asia Publishing House Bombay, 1961.

F.A.O., Manual of Sericulture—1, Mulberry Cultivation, Oxford & IBH Publishing Company, (Pvt.), Ltd., New Delhi. 1993.

——, Manual of Sericulture-2 Silk Worm Reading, Oxford & IBH Publishing Company, (Pvt.) Ltd., New Delhi, 1993.

——, Sericulture Training Manual, Oxford & IBH Publishing Company, New Delhi, 1994.

Ganga, G., & Sulochana Chetty, J., An Introduction to Sericulture, Oxford & IBH Publishing Company, (Pvt.) Ltd., New Delhi, 1991.

Ghosh, Alok, Indian Economy, 1988-89. It's Nature and Problems, The World Press Private Ltd., Calcutta, 1988.

Ghosh C.C., Silk Production and Weaving in Indian, CSIR, New Delhi, 1949.

Gopalachar, A.R.S., Three Decade of Sericulture Progress, CSB, Bangalore, 1978.

Giri, V.V., Jobs for Millions, 1970.

Gyan Chand, Population in Perspective, 1972.

Hanumappa, H.G., Sericulture for Rural Development, Himalaya Publishing House, Bombay, 1986.

——, Sericulture Society and Economy, Himalaya Publishing House, Bombay, 1993.

Harpal Singh, Y., Project for the Development of Sericulture, National Institute of Bank Management, Bombay.

Iqbal A. Badar, Financing of Agro-Industrial Development in India, Kmar Publications, Aligarh, 1979.

Jagdananad Jha, Khadi and Village Industries in Economic Development, Deep & Deep Publications, New Delhi, 1990.

Jha, D.N., Planning and Agricultural Development, Vikas Publications, New Delhi, 1974.

Jolly, M.S., Appropriate Sericulture Techniques, Director, International Centre for Training & Research in Tropical Sericulture, Mysore, 1987.

Jolly, M.S., Chowdhury, S.N., & Sen, S.K., Non-Mulberry Sericulture in India, Central Silk Board, Bombay, 1975.

Krishna Swamy, S., Mulberry Cultivation in South India, CSRTI, CSB, Govt. of India, Ministry of Textiles, Bangalore, 1986.

——, Improved Method of Rearing Young Age (Chawkie) Silk Worms, CSRTI, CSB, Govt. of India, Ministry of Textiles, Bangalore, 1986.

——, New Technology of Silk Worm Rearing, CSRTI, CSB, Govt. of India, Ministry of Textiles, Bangalore, 1986.

——, Economics of Sericulture Under Irrigated Conditions, CSRTI, CSB, Govt. of India, Ministry of Textiles, Bangalore, 1986.

Koshy, K.D., Silk Exports and Development, Ashish Publishing House, New Delhi, 1993.

Momoria, C.B., Agricultural Problems of India, Kitab Mahal, Allahabad, 1984.

Michael P. Todaro, Economic Development in the Third World, Orient Longman, Hyderabad, 1991.

Misra, R.P., Rural Industrialisation inThird World Countries, Sterling Publishers, (Pvt.) Ltd., New Delhi, 1985.

Mukerji, N.G., Hand Book of Sericulture, Bengal Secretariat Book Department, Calcutta, 1906.

Myrdal Gunnar, Asian Drama—An Enquiry into the Poverty of Nations, The Twentieth Century Fund, Inc., Vol. 11, London, 1968.

Mysore Silk Association, Silk Worm Rearing and Diseases of Silk Worms, Bangalore, 1956.

Nanavathy M. Mahesh, Silk-Production, Processing and Marketing, Wiley Eastern Limited, New Delhi, 1990.

Narayana, D.L., Economics of Sericulture in Rayalaseema, Technical, S.V. University, Tirupati, 1979.

——, Employment and Economic Growth, Madhurai Kamaraj University, Madhurai, 1970.

——, Entrepreneurship and Agricultural Development, Indian Institute for Asian Studies, Bombay, 1966.

Raj Purohit, A.R., & Govinda Raj, K.V. Employment and Income in Sericulture, Shiny Publications, Bangalore, 1981.

Rao, R.V., Rural Industrialisation in India, Classical Publishers, New Delhi, 1973.

Ramakrishna Sharma, Industrial Development of Andhra Pradesh, Himalaya Publishing House, Bombay, 1982.

Ramana, D.V., Economics of Sericulture and Silk Industry in India, Deep & Deep Publications, New Delhi, 1987.

Ramanadham, V.V., Economics of Andhra Pradesh, Asia Publishing House, Bombay, 1959.

Rowley, R.C., Economics of Silk Industry, P.S. King & Song Ltd., London, 1919.

Sadhak, H., Industrial Development in Backward Regions in India, Chugh Publications, Allahabad, 1986.

Santha Raj Kumar S.B., Silk Handloom Industry in Andhra Pradesh, Sonali Printers, Pune, 1986.

Sinha Sanjay, The Development of India Silk, Oxford & IBH Publishing Company (Pvt.) Ltd., New Delhi, 1986.

Thammanna. N., & Hand Book of Silk Technology, Wiley Sonwalkar Eastern Limited, New Delhi, 1993.

Tazinma, Y., Sericulture Industry in India, CSB, Bombay.

Ullal, S.R. & Narasimhanna, M.N., Hand Book of Practical Sericulture, CSB, Bombay, 1978.

Venkata Narasaiah, P., Sericulture in India, Ashish Publishing House, New Delhi, 1992.

Venkaish, V., Impact of Agrio-Based Industries on Rural Economy, Himalaya Publishing House, Bombay, 1987.

Reports

Central Silk Board, Souvenir, International Congress of Tropical Sericulture Practices (18-23), February, Bangalore, 1985.

——, Proceedings of the International Congress on Tropical Sericulture Practices (18-23), February, Bangalore, 1988.

——, Statistical Biennial, 1986.

Central Silk Board, Statistical Biennial, 1988.

——, Statistical Biennial, 1990.

——, Statistical Biennial, 1992.

——, Sericulture Development Programme During VIII Plan (1992-97) and Annual Plan 1992-93 Under Central Sector, Bangalore, 1991.

——, The NSP Newsletter, A Monthly Publication of the National Sericulture Project, Vol. 1, Nos. 1-12, Bangalore, 1991.

——, A Note on Present Status of Indian Sericulture, Its Silk Production and Exports, Bangalore, 1987-88.

CSR & TI, Seridoc, A Quarterly Document of Sericultural Research and Training Institute, Mysore.

Centre for Planning & Development Studies Evaluation of the Impact of Drought Prone Areas Programme in Anantapur District, 1987, Anantapur (unpublished report).

Centre for Rayalaseema Development Studies, Development of Sericulture and its Impact on Cropping pattern in Rayalaseema Districts S.K.University, Anantapur (Unpublished Report).

T. Chandra Reddy, Impact of Sericulture Industry on Income and Employment in Rural Area of Chittoor district of Andhra Pradesh (unpublished Ph.D. thesis submitted to U.A.S., Bangalore, 1987).

Government of Andhra Pradesh, Planning and Development of Backward Regions—A Case Study in Rayalaseema, Vol. I.

——, Annual Administration Reports 1980-81 to 1993-94, Dept. of Sericulture, Hyderabad.

Govt. of Andhra Pradesh, A Note on Implementation of National Sericulture Projcet in A.P. (Summary and Progress)—Dept. of Sericulture, Hyderabad, 1991.

——, Hand Book of Statistics, Anantapur District, CPO, Anantapur, 1991-93.

——, Hand Book of Statistics, Chittoor District, 1992-93 CPO, Chittoor.

——, Hand Book of Statistics, Kurnool District, 1992-93 CPO, Kurnool.

——, Hand Book of Statistics, Cuddapah District, 1991-93 CPO, Cuddapah.

——, Pattu Sravanthi, A Quarterly Document of the Dept. of Sericulture, Hyderabad.

——, Action Plan for Women in Sericulture in A.P., Dept. of Sericulture, Hyderabad.

——, Andhra Pradesh State Gazetteer, Hyderabad.

——, Sericulture Development under DPAP; Anantapur District, Dept. of Sericulture Anantapur, 1987.

——, New Horizon for Sericulture in Andhra Pradesh, Dept. of Textiles and Handloom, Hyderabad, 1976.

——, Brief Note on the Development of Sericulture in Anantapur District, Dept. of Sericulture, Anantapur, 1994.

——, Status Paper on Sericulture in Andhra Predesh, Orientation Programme Sericulture for Bankers from A.P. (24th June-1st July) 1991. Dept. of Sericulture, Hyderabad, 1991.

——, Crop and Season Reports, Directorate of Economics and Statistics, Hyderabad, 1980-81 to 1993-94.

——, Master Plan for Sericulture Development in Andhra Pradesh (1981-82 to 1985-86).

——, Block Plans 1980-81, Anantapur District, Intensive Development of Block Under the Integrated Rural Development Programme.

——, Anantapur District Gazetter, Hyderabad.

——, Chittoor District Gazetter, Hyderabad.

——, Kurnool District Gazetter, Hyderabad.

——, Cuddapah District Gazetter, Hyderabad.

——, Credit Plan for Sericulture in Andhra Pradesh, Department of Handlooms and Textiles, 1978.

——, District Plans Under Drought Prone Areas Programme, Integrated Rural Development Programme and District Rural Development Agency Programme, Anantapur District.

——, A Brief Note on World Bank Assistance Programmes, Directorate of Sericulture, Hyderabad, 1988.

——, A Brief Note on Sericulture Project Under Indo-Swiss Programmes, Dept. of Sericulture, Anantapur, 1989.

——, Report on Swiss Assistance Programmes, Dept. of Sericulture, Anantapur, 1989.

——, Report on S.C. Action Plan, 1984-85 to 1988-89, Dept. of Sericulture, Anantapur.

——, Industrial Profile of Anantapur District, General Manager, District Industries Centre, Anantapur, 1987.

——, Progress Reports, 1980-81 to 1993-94, Dept. of Sericulture, Anantapur.

Government of India, Drought Prone Areas Programme, Ministry of Agriculture, Department of Rural Development, New Delhi, 1978.

——, First Five Years Plan—A Draft Out Line, Planning Commission, New Delhi, 1991.

——, Eighth Five Years Plan, (1992-97), Vol. I, & Vol. II Planning Commission, New Delhi, 1991.

——, Census of India, 1991, Series 1 and 2, District Census Hand Book, Anantapur District Parts XIII- A & B, Village, Town Directory, Village, Town-wise Primary Abstract.

——, Report on Financing of Small Scale Industries, State Bank of India Study Team.

Government of Karnataka, Karnataka State Gazetter, Bangalore.

Indian Institute of Economics, Techno Economic Survey of the Potentialities for the Development of Sericulture Industry in Andhra Pradesh, 1972. (VII Published).

International Trade, Silk Review, 1990-A Survey of Centre UNCTAD/ GATT International Trends in Production and Trade, Geneva.

Institute for Social and Economic Change, Problems and Prospects of Sericulture, A Study in Some Villages in Two Districts of T.N., J. Acharya and others, (Beneficiary Assessment Report), Bangalore, 1991.

National Institute of, Block Plan in the District Frame. A Rural.

Govt. of Andhra Pradesh, Progress Reports, 1980-81 to 1993-94, Dept. of Sericulture, Anantapur.

National Institute of Development, Block Plan in the District Frame, A Rural Development Plan for Madakasira Block in Anantapur District, Andhra Pradesh, 1979.

National Commission on Agriculture, Report of the National Commission on Agriculture, Part III, Crop Production, Sericulture and Agriculture, New Delhi, 1976.

Prasad, B., Studies on Reproductive Physiology of Silkworm Bombays Mori (L) in Relation to Organic Reserves of the Mulberry Leaves (Unpublished Thesis).

Reserve Bank of India, Report on Financing the Crash Programme for the Development of Sericulture in Karnataka, Bombay, 1974.

The Hindu, Survey on India Agriculture, Year Books 1989 to 1998.

Tariff Board, (Govt. of India), Report of the Indian Tariff Board Regarding Granting of Protection to Sericulture Industry, Manager, Govt. of India Press, Calcutta 1940.

Tariff Commission the (Govt. of India), Report on the Continuance of Protection to Sericulture Industry, Bombay, 1974.

Tropical Development Hangh, Research Institute, The World Market for Silk, Peter Green and London, 1987.

Articles

Abdul Majid, 'Dramatic Development in Andhra Sericulture' *Indian Silk*, Vol. XVII, No.6, October, 1978.

Arun Chandra, Guha, 'The Urgency of Cottage Industries', *Khadi Gramodyog*, The Journal of Rural Economics, Vol. XX V, No. 2, November, 1978.

Ashal, M.M., 'Package and Practices for Mulberry Cultivation Under Temperate Conditions', *Indian Silk*, Vol. 29., June. 1990.

Balasubramanian, V., 'Sericulture as a High Employment Oriented Industry', *Indian Silk*, Vol. XXV, No. 6, October, 1986.

Balwinder Singh, 'Impact of Local Points on Marketing of Farm Produce', *Kurushetra*, 29(4), April, 1981.

Benchamin, K.V., & Rural Jolly. M.S., 'Employment and Income Generation in the Areas Through Sericulture', *Indian Silk*, Vol. XXV, June, 1987.

Benchamin, K.V., 'Sericulture in Bangladesh', *Indian Silk*, Vol. 32, No. 6, 1993.

Bhatikar, A.P., 'Sericulture and Rural Industrialisation (Part II)', *Indian Silk*, Vol. XXIV, No. 3, July, 1985.

Bongale, V.D., 'Mulberry Varieties in the Context of Indian Sericulture', *Indian Silk*, Vol. 29, No. 2, June, 1990.

Boraiah, G., 'Establishment of Germplasm Bank in Mulberry and the Evaluation of Mulberry, Varieties,', *Lecturers on Sericulture*, Suramya Publications, Bangalore, 1986.

——, 'Mulberry Cultivation', *Lecturers on Sericulture*, Suramya Publications, Bangalore, 1986.

Central Sericulture Research & Training Institute, Mysore, 'Mulberry Cultivation Under Rainfed Conditions A Challenge that Should be Met' *Indian Silk*, Vol. XXV, No. 81, December, 1987.

Chowkidar, V.V. & May, Pai, M.S., 'Sericulture Development', *Economic Times* 1976.

Datta, R.K., 'Progress and Prospects of Sericulture in India Under the Central Sector', *Indian Silk*, Vol. XXV, No. 9, January, 1987.

Dastagir, S.R., 'Sericulture', *Land Bank Journal*, Vol. XVIII, June , 1980, Issue-VI.

Dayananda Reddy, R., 'Farmers Training Programme—An Effective Tool for the Transfer of Technology to the Field', *Indian Silk*, Vol. XXVIII, No. 8, December, 1989.

Dantwala, M.L., 'Rural Employment—Facts and Issues', *Economics and Political Weekly*, Vol. XIV, No. 2, June 23, 1979.

Devasurappa, L., 'Silk Industry in Karnataka', *Reshme Krushi* Journal, January, 1980.

Deshmukh, 'Can Poverty be Removed From Our Countgry' *Bharateeya Vikas*, Vol. No. 2, October-December, 1980.

Editor, 'The Versatality of Indian Silks', *Indian Silk*, Vol. VIII, No. 9, 1969.

——, 'Indo-Japanese Silk Accord Under World Bank Programme', *Indian Silk*, Vol. XIX, No.10, February, 1981.

——, 'Sericulture in India—Great Expectations and Great Challenges', *Indian Silk*, Vol. XXVI, No.9, January, 1988.

——, 'Chinese Leader Favours Silk Accord with India', *Indian Silk* Vol. XIX, No. II, March, 1981.

——, 'Reports on Japan Sericulture', *Indian Silk*, Vol. XVI, No. 4, August, 1977.

——, 'Sericulture Comes of Age in India', *Indian Silk*, Vol. XXVI, No. 1, May, 1989.

——, 'The Triumph of Sericulture in Andhra Predesh *Indian Silk*, Vol. XXX, No. 9, January, 1992.

Gopalachar, A.R.S., 'March of Sericulture Industry During Post Independence Era', *Indian Silk*, Vol. XI, No. 4, August, 1972.

George Fernandes, 'India Can Treble Her Silk Output', *Indian Silk*, Vol. XVII, No. 7, November, 1978.

Hanumappa H.G. & Errappa, S., Economic Issues in Sericulture, Study of K arnataka, Economic and Political Weekly, August, 1985.

——, 'The Saga of Sericulture in the Princely State of Mysore', *Indian Silk*, Vol. XXVIII, No. 4, August, 1989.

Hanumappa, H.G., 'Rural Development—Projects Some Experiences with Karnataka Sericulture Project'—*Lectures on Sericulture*, Suramya Publications, Bangalore.

Hanumappa, H.G & Mangala, Issue in Sericulture Activities—Macro Prospectives. Lectures on Sericulture, Suramya Publications, Bangalore, 1986.

Iqaubal, A.,·Badar, 'Performances and Prospects', *Khadi Gramodyog*, Vol. XXVII, No.11, August, 1981.

Jyoteeswar Patlik, 'Silk Worm Reading—A New Approach', *Yojana*, September, 1976.

Jayaswal, K.A. & Datta, R.K., 'Some Popular Milberry Silk Worm Races in India', *India Silk*, Vol. XXXI, No. 9, January, 1993.

Kasivishvanathan, K., 'The Role of the State Khadi and Village Industries Board', *Indian Silk*, Vol. XXIX, No. 4, August, 1990

Krishna Swamy, S., 'A New Strategy for Producing High Grade Raw Silk in Mysore', *Indian Silk*, Vol. X, No. 1, 1971.

——, 'Progress, Prospects and Problems of Sericulture in India', *Indian Silk*, Vol. XXV, No. 12 & 1, April and May 14, 1986.

Kamaraju Panthulu, N., *'Development of Sericulture in Rayalaseema'*, Khadi Gramodyog, March, 1977.

Kanna, V.K., 'Will China Resume the Silk Exports', Indian Silk, Vol. XXVII, No. 7, November, 1988.

Lakshman. S., & Thiagarajan, V., 'Growth of Indian Silk Export—Analitical', Approach Agriculture Situation in India, May, 1991.

Lele, D.V., An Appraisal to Sericulture', Khadi Gramodyog, Vol. XVII, December, 1979.

Manjeet, S. Jooly, 'Chawkie Rearing-Concept Organisation and Management' Indian Silk, Vol. XV, January, 1987.

Mira Madan and Satyawati Sharma, 'Mulberry Sericulture in the Non-Traditional Areas', Indian Silk, Vol. XXX, No. 5, October, 1991.

Muneer Pasha, M.D, 'Swiss Aid to the Mulberry Sericulture Development in Andhra Pradesh and Tamil Nadu, Indian Silk, Vol. XXVII, No. 3, July, 1988.

——, "The Road to Prosperity, Development of Bivoltine Sericulture in India, Indian Silk, Vol. XXVII, No. 8, Decembesr, 1988.

Narasimhanna, M.N., 'A Sound Sed Organisation for Sericulture Industry', Lecturers on Sericulture, Suramya Publications, Bangalore, 1986.

——, 'Silk Worm Seed Production', Lectures on Sericulture, Suramya Publications, Bangalore, 1986.

Naidu, E.M. & Naidu, B.J., 'Sericulture and Rural Development in Seventh Plan', *Southern Economist'*, November, 1984.

Narayana, D.L., 'Migration and Agriculture Development', *Khadi Gramodyog*, July, 1966.

Patel, K.V., 'Sericulture—An Instrument of Change- Some Gross Root Level Lessons', *Indian Silk*, Vol. XXXI, No. 3, July 1992.

Patel, A.R., 'Sericulture—A Labour—Intensive Industry *Khadi Gramodyog*, Vo. XXII, December, 1976.

Periswamy.K, 'Problems and Prospects of Sericulture', *Indian Silk*, Vol. XVI, No. 6, October, 1977.

Rao, G.V.K., Repeat World Bank Sericulture Project for Speedy Progress', *Indian Silk*, Vol. XXIII, No. 10 & 11 No. 10 & 11, February, 1985.

Rao, M.N., 'Economics of Sericulture', *Khadi Gramodyog*, Vol. XXII, June, 1977.

Ramakrishna, 'Sericulture: An Evaluation of Impact', *The Economics Times*, November, 1987.

Rao, G.V.K & Tharmarakshi, 'Some Aspects of Growth in Indian Agriculture', *Economics and Political Weekly*, Vol. XIII, No. 51 & 52, December, 1978.

Rao S.K & Amul Snyal, 'On Promoting Employment Through Labour Intensity of Techniques' *Economic and Political Weekly*, Vol. XIII, No. 6 & 7, Annual Number, 1978.

Ranganatha Rao, K., 'A Reportorial of an Inspiring Tour in Andhra Pradesh', *Indian Silk*, Vol. XVI, No. 3, 1977.

Royale, J.G., 'Silk Culture in India', *Indian Silk*, Vol. XXV, No. 2, June, 1986.

Sanjay Sinha, 'Development Impact of Silk Production—A Wealth of Opportunities', *Economics and Political Weekly*, Vol. XXIV, No. 3, January, 1989.

Sankar, A., 'Extension Agent—An Efficient Medium for the Spread of Sericulture', *Indian Silk*, Vol. XXV, No. 10, February, 1987.

Sinha, J.N., 'Rural Employment Planning—Dimenstions and Constraints', *Economic and Political Weekly*, Vol. XIII, No. 6 & 7, Annual Number, 1987.

Shivananda, H.K, 'Agricultural Markets and Cocoon Markets in Karnataka', *Indian Silk*, Vol. XXVI, No. 10, September, 1987.

Shoban Babu, E., 'Economics of Silk Reeling and Twisting Units in Anantapur', *Indian Silk*, Vo. XXV, No. 10, February, 1987.

——, 'Sericulture Industry Can Work Wonders for the Drought-Prone Area of Anantapur District', Indian Silk, Vol. XXVII, No. 7, November, 1988.

Susheelamma, B.N. & Benchamin, K.V. 'Mulberry Tree Cultivation in Bangladesh', *Indian Silk*, Vol. 34, No. 2, June, 1995.

Sonwalkar, T.N., 'Factorss Influencing Reeling Efficiency', *Indian Silk*, Vol. XVI, No. 6, October, 1977.

Thnang Dahnan, Linshi Xian & Lilong, 'Sericulture Production Strategies in the 21st Century', Linshi *Indian Silk*, Vol. 33, No. 8.

Thimmaiah, G & Rao, V.M., 'Problems and Prospects of Sericulture Development in Karnataka—A Field Review', *Sericulture for Rural Development*.

Tomy Philip, 'Why Silk is Precious', *Indian Silk*, Vol, XXVII, No. 9, January, 1989.

Index

F

G

H

I

J

K

L

M